Testimonials

The Another Touch of Glory Ministries Training Center of Prophetic People and the book, *Raising Prophets of Character,* have served and still serve as one of the most referenced resources that pertain to the establishing of the prophetic work at Springs of Living Water Ministries, Inc. The integrity of the multi-faceted gift of the prophet is maintained through character development, accuracy, and accountability. As a prophet, I find that the training center and the book keep me encouraged, refreshed, challenged, and accountable, and therefore, growing in the "grace." For the prophetic people whom the Lord has entrusted to our care and tasked us to equip and "father," our having this resource serves as quality affirmation and confirmation that we are on point.

--Pastor Joseph and Senior Prophet LaTanya Jimerson
Springs of Living Waters Ministries, Inc.
Waldorf, Maryland

Raising Prophets of Character is more than a book to read – it is a training manual and instructional tool that every church, ministry, and leader must have to move their churches, ministries, and leadership to a 21st century Apostolic and Prophetic House. This book is a historical, revelational, biblical, theological, and academic reference for the 21st century focused leader. This great tool and training manual is a must for training centers for prophets and makes reference to the transition, transference, transformation, testing, and triumphs that will help to make and shape the prophets for this season. It also gives further insight into what it takes for a prophet to become who he or she really is in Christ, the community, and the countries that have long awaited to hear a pure and precious word from the mouth of the prophet.

--Bishop H. Eugene Bellinger
Cathedral of the Covenant Church
Columbus, Ohio

"Then the word of the Lord came unto me saying, Before I formed thee in the belly I knew thee; and before thou camest forth out of the womb I sanctified thee, and I ordained thee a prophet unto the nations" (Jeremiah 1:4-5). "And he gave some, apostles; and some, prophets; and some evangelists; and some, pastors and teachers; For the perfecting of the body of Christ" (Ephesians 4:11-12). These scriptures became the very life of my present as my future was being unfolded. Prophet Rodney Walker, the founder and visionary of the Another Touch of Glory Ministries Training Center of Prophetic People, fathered these very words in my life. After walking closely with him as a prophet in the making, and completing three levels of the training, my life has become so joined with destiny and purpose. His teachings from *Raising Prophets of Character* gave me an arsenal for the prophetic, the prophet, prophecy, and the prophet's assignment. The training center and Prophet Walker's teachings are a must for those who need answers to difficult questions. Do prophets exist today? Am I a prophet? What is a prophet? What is my assignment as a prophet? Most of all, where do I fit in the body of Christ as a prophet? If there has ever been a time for the prophet to come forth and be fathered, that time is now. I encourage all who believe the prophetic call is on their life to attend the school of prophets. You will not be disappointed, and your life will be transformed forever. Prophet Walker is one of the greatest father prophets and teachers of the prophetic of our times.

--Prophet Alvin E. Smith
Pastor, Son Light Covenant Church
Crestview, Florida

Becoming a Proven Prophetic Voice

Bishop R.S. Walker

Published by Bishop R.S. Walker Ministries formerly Another Touch of Glory Press
2760 Crain Highway
Waldorf, Maryland 20601
Voice (301-843-9267) - (877-200-8967)
Fax (240-585-7093)
Web address: http://www.bishoprswalker.com
E-mail: admin@bishoprswalker.com

ISBN-13: 978-0692435090
ISBN-10: 0692435093

Published in the United States of America

Table of Contents

Foreword

I think Rodney has touched the heart of God relative to this apostolic and prophetic season that we now embrace. The voice of the Lord is clarion. Not only are we hearing Him speak, we are seeing what He's saying. To miss the truth of His message is to be lost. Who can afford to take this risk?

I'm convinced that as we see the end approach, the prophetic move of the Lord will only escalate. Consequently, we must increase our sensitivity to hear exactly what He is saying, the way He says it, and in the context that He wants us to comprehend His truth. Any deviation from the truth becomes error. Yet there are many exercising this gift of prophecy with seemingly little or no concern for the exactness of His words or recognition of divine patterns that often serve as prerequisites of certain promised blessings. For these prophets, every promise seems to be unconditional, as if God is just going to do this, that or the other, anyhow. When what has been prophesied fails to come to pass, the poor expectant becomes utterly disappointed and often cynical about the Church and its God.

One way to reduce the "at-risk" Believer who floats from church to church and from one conference to the next seeking "a word," is to bring integrity back to the position of the prophet. The real prophet of the Lord must not be intimidated when there's a need to prophesy "woes" as well as blessings. Likewise, the prophet must know the ways of God, so as not to contradict the patterns and prerequisites that are set forth in the Scriptures before blessings can flow. Prophets often know the thin line between truth and error. One step in the wrong direction may indeed sound better, but could in fact be the difference between truth and error. To avoid leading those who are hungry for a word, into error, we must raise up prophets who see "character" as an absolutely indispensable component. The key is to remember that we do not speak our own thoughts or ideas; we have a God-given responsibility to speak only what the Lord says, the way the Lord says it, and in the same context in which He gives it. *Lord, help us to raise up prophets with character!*

As key leaders and mentors in ministry, we must take responsibility to raise up prophets after the heart of God. Prophesying blessings must not become a fad or an occasion to get people hyped. Let's remember that it's knowing the truth, that makes us free! Anything else spells bondages and ultimately, destruction.

Bishop Ralph L. Dennis
Senior Pastor, Kingdom Worship Center
and Columbia Family Worship Center
Baltimore, Maryland

About the Author

Prophet Walker is a native of Washington, D.C. where he received his early education in the District of Columbia's public school system. He is a graduate of Jericho Christian Training College and of the Spirit of Truth Institute where he received his Doctor of Divinity degree.

Prophet Walker is spiritually covered by and accountable to Bishop/Apostle Ralph L. Dennis of Kingdom Worship Center in Baltimore, Maryland, Bishop Dennis is the spiritual son of Dr. Mark Hanby. In July of 1998, Kingdom Fellowship Covenant Ministries, of which he is a Covenant Set Gift, bestowed upon Prophet Walker the Apostolic Appointment to the work of Chief Elder/Overseer. As such, Prophet Walker provided assigned regional oversight in the ministry of the Prophetic ascension gift. God has so blessed him with versatile instructors, mentors and a spiritual father, who have collectively developed him into the well-rounded, well-grounded, teaching prophet of God as you will experience through his teaching, preaching and ministry. In addition to his many assignments, he is the founder and Senior Pastor of Heritage Church International, formerly known and established as God Is In Control Church in 1990. God furthered the vision and led Bishop-Elect Rodney Walker to Change the name to Heritage Church International in April 2008 and is currently located in Waldorf, MD at 2772 Crain Highway. He also serves as the Overseer of Heritage Church International and covers a number of churches, both nationally and internationally which does not exclude other para-church ministries and businesses within the United States.

Prophet Walker founded ATOG School of The Prophets. The school has now gone into much of the United States of America. This ATOG School of the Prophets has an eye for global impact and has set as its goal to have a presence in every state and country. Presently, Another Touch of Glory Ministries has schools operating in Waldorf, and Baltimore, MD, Raleigh, Wilson, Sanford, Brown Summit and Kinston NC and in Abuja, Nigeria. In addition to its physical school locations, Another Touch of Glory School of the Prophets offers correspondence courses north, south, east and west of the United States - not to exclude Another Touch of Glory School of the Prophets in Nigeria, Africa.

Prophet Walker has also raised a body of Prophetic Presbyters who assist him in managing the great assignment God has set to his hands... In addition, Prophet Walker is the author, publisher, and conference speaker... Due to his God-given charge to train those who are in the Five-Fold Ministry, Prophet Walker has a ministerial staff that exceeds the size of most ministries of the same magnitude.

Ephesians 4 is foundational to his charge and calling. However, one of his dearest accomplishments is that of being a devoted husband to his lovely wife, Elder Betty Walker, and a loving father to his ten wonderful children. Prophet Walker's ultimate goal is to fulfill all that God has purposed for his life and for those placed in his prophetic and pastoral care. His love for God is evident through his preaching, teaching and zeal in ministry. You will experience God through this man of God...†

Declaring Faith in all the Earth!

The Five Seasons of the Prophet

A. Season of Becoming (Metamorphosis)
B. Season of Challenged Purpose
C. Season of Maturity
D. Season of Equipping
E. Process of Release

SEASON #1
THE SEASON OF BECOMING

meta|mor|pho|sis

n., pl. -[**ses** (-sez) < Gr *metamorphosis* < *metamorphoun,* to transform, transfigure < *meta,* over (see META-) + *morphe,* form, shape]

1. *a* change of form, shape, structure, or substance; transformation, the form resulting from such change

2. a marked or complete change of character, appearance, condition, etc.

3. *Biol.* a change in form, structure, or function as a result of development; specif., the physical transformation, more or less sudden, undergone by various animals during development after the embryonic state, as of the larva of an insect to the pupa and the pupa to the adult, or of the tadpole to the frog

4. *Med.* a pathological change of form of some tissues

--taken from *Webster's New World Dictionary*

CHAPTER 1

The Metamorphosis Process

Metamorphosis: 1. A change of physical form, structure, or substance especially by supernatural means. 2. A striking alteration in appearance, character, or circumstances. 3. A marked and more or less abrupt developmental change in the form or structure of an animal (as a butterfly or a frog) occurring subsequent to birth or hatching.

—taken from *Webster's Collegiate Dictionary*

It's time for the change...

I magine, all of this time you have existed as no one but yourself. You have been whatever your name happens to be. That's all that you have been all of this time. Now that you've come into the knowledge of Jesus, you are still the same person you were, but with Jesus in your life. You've now become conscious of who you are to be in Him; but massive changes have not yet taken place because you have not yet entered ministry.

Because you have not entered ministry at this point, your proverbial boat remains calm and steady. There is no shaking. In fact, your boat has never really been shaken before. In contrast, the minute you accept ministry, your boat begins to shake and rock. It is at this very moment that you begin to become someone you've never known before.

Jesus hand-picked some people whom He absolutely shook! In essence, He disturbed the foundations of who they were. Those who had been chosen figured that they were simply acknowledging a call. Well, what happens when you acknowledge a call?

Remember, you said that you would go; you said that you would do "this," and you said that you would do "that." These declarations initiated the process of "metamorphosis." The "course of change" has now found you. The person you've known all of this time now begins to become obsolete and foreign to you. You must learn, now, that you cannot make decisions based on this person any longer. Your decisions must be made according to the person whom you are becoming, even though you don't know *what* you are becoming.

The process of metamorphosis may best be seen in the life of the tadpole. Tadpoles were born in the creek. These little guys have lived the simple life. They just swim around the creek to their hearts' content. They grow and grow and become bigger and bigger, but they still have that tail and continue to swim around their precious little creek.

If you watch tadpoles long enough, however, you'll find that they will begin to grow legs. Even with these newly formed legs, they proceed to swim around the creek. They have legs, but they're still swimming!

The problem is that the tadpole is actually becoming. It is becoming what it's never been before in its life. Eventually, though, we all know that this tadpole and all of the other tadpoles will develop into a frog. As a tadpole, it doesn't look like a frog at all. But, change begins to set in. The tadpole starts to take on another physical form or structure. Not only will its form change, but its operation will change as well.

The tadpole, at the set time and the set moment, will lose its tail and mature from wagging its tail to leaping. It will leap farther than anything else in the water can leap. Nonetheless, this is not the limit of the tadpole's transformation. As a tadpole, it was confined to the boundaries of water. As a frog, the tadpole becomes amphibious.

The frog is an amazing creature. You see, the frog is not confined to the water. It can go underwater and emerge onto dry land at its leisure. But let us not forget, it didn't start out as a frog; its life began as a tadpole. The process of metamorphosis took place, and the tadpole became something it had never been before. The frog began to do things it had never done before. The frog became something it had never known before.

Likewise, the caterpillar that had only been accustomed to crawling around on the ground also meets change. It had only been a caterpillar that had also been confined to a particular area. It had never known the experience of flying, and at the set time and at the set moment, it became of such that can fly. How does this really happen? Why does it even happen? The answer: metamorphosis.

You and I are like tadpoles and caterpillars. We are becoming what we've never been before, and we don't understand it. We don't understand what's happening on the inside of us. Yet, we are still becoming.

It is the will of God that we become what He desires that we become. Why do you think that some of us fail to become? Has a tadpole, which was born a tadpole, ever set its will to not become a frog? Has a caterpillar, which was born a caterpillar, ever set its will to not become a butterfly? Absolutely not! Neither of these creatures had a choice in their metamorphosis process. We, on the other hand, do have a choice.

We must realize that we are the only ones that were created in the image and the likeness of God. No other creature on the planet has been so privileged. We have been given a will that we can set to submit to the plan of God or to fight against the plan of God.

We make the decision, as prophets, prophetic people, and men and women of God to become. Sure, the road to becoming is very painful. Conversely, the road to resistance is even more painful. The road to becoming is laden with benefits. The road to resistance is laden with penalties. Pain is inevitable, but the pain that you prefer is your decision alone. Make the right choice.

The choice to become is left totally in your hands. The process of metamorphosis is designed to develop you into what is in the mind of God, as it concerns you. If you yield to the process, the pain will prove to be worthwhile, and becoming what God has destined you to be will be unavoidable. If you resist the process, the pain will prove to be unbearable and unnecessary, and what God has destined you to be will follow you to your grave.

– THE TRIUNE MAN –

It is the other part of you that gets in the way. Before I speak a word into your life, I have to assess your situation. Where have you been? Before you give someone "a word" that God is not going to honor you have to know where they are. I can come to you and tell you that God is getting ready to shift your whole world, and that He is getting ready to bring you into promise. Well promise may mean that you are now coming into the fullness of what God has already said, but you may be (in this particular season) faltering in your tithing. That means that you are faltering in your prophetic exchange. So now no matter what I say, it is not going to happen until we can get you across this particular area. Then, even after you start tithing, you repent, and you get that part right--you still may have a season where you are not going to come into it. It depends on what you did with the ten percent--because you may have opened up another season that we have to wait to die out, before fulfillment of what God said can come to pass.

If you are a seer, you can only see in a concentrated area where you have authority in your region. Once we move pass your area, then we need a prophet. If a prophet is standing near trying to prophesy them into their future, he must assess their past. How much stuff did they mess up that will now possibly hinder what they are going to be able to do in their future? So we need to be able to see and assess what we need to be able to fix up. Can we just annihilate all of that? Sometimes we can and sometimes we cannot. It is for the prophet to be able to see what we can and what we cannot annihilate.

NOTE

SEASON #2
SEASON OF CHALLENGED PURPOSE

chal lenge

n. ME & OFr *chalenge*, accusation, claim, dispute < L *calumnia*, CALUMNY

1. a demand for identification [a sentry gave the *challenge*]

2. a calling into question; a demanding of proof, explanation, etc.[a *challenge* of the premises of an argument]

3. a call or dare to take part in a duel, contest, etc.

4. anything, as a demanding task, that calls for special effort or dedication

5. an objection to a vote or to someone's right to vote

6. *Law* a formal objection or exception to a person who has been chosen as a prospective juror

—taken from *Webster's New World Dictionary*

There is a season that the prophet goes through, when he or she is challenged to see what level of pressure he or she is able to handle. If the prophet is unable to handle pressure in this season, he or she is disqualified for his or her readiness for the next season.

No one just goes to the next season. There has to be a qualifying process. You must be made ready for what is next. Notice our definition of "challenge." Through this season there will be accusation, claim, and dispute. The question is can you handle those kinds of

"For our light affliction, which is but for a moment, worketh for us a far more exceeding and eternal weight of glory; While we look not at the things which are seen, but at the things which are not seen: for the things which are seen are temporal; but the things which are not seen are eternal."
2 Corinthians 4:17

things? Remember, you are called and anointed to solve problems. In the season of challenge, you learn these kinds of things, but only if you are a catcher. If the best you can do is learn from lessons taught verbally, then the season of challenge will defeat you. The season of challenge is a season during which you learn to catch lessons, more than being verbally taught them. Some things are taught; other things are caught. The season of challenge is a catching season.

Being accused is the norm in this season. Accusation is not something that is designed to kill you, but to grow you. Many of these kinds of opportunities come to us as prophets and apostles, but we forfeit the growth by not allowing it to work for us.

The thing we must master is that there are things that work for us, but the criterion is, "We look not at what is seen, but at what is not seen." Let the season of challenge work for you a far more exceeding weight of glory.

CHAPTER 2

Understanding the Father-Son Relationship

The Father-Son Relationship from an Earthly Perspective

The concept of the father-son relationship has been widely misunderstood. The misunderstanding of this vitally important relationship has surfaced in part because of the earthly perspective from which we've drawn our understanding.

The concept of fathering did not originate from an earthly pattern. Yet when we think of the spiritual father or the spiritual son, we confine our thinking to earthly models that we have either observed or experienced. This earthly perspective of the father-son relationship causes us to experience difficulties and conflicts, when we attempt to initiate and maintain spiritual father-son relationships from this perspective. We have made the concept of the father-son relationship too earthly.

From an earthly perspective, we are governed by gender-based assignments. Gender-based assignments require a male and female in order to produce a son. In other words, if I have a father, I must also have a mother. Therefore, if I am to have a spiritual father, I must also have a spiritual mother. Moreover, if we attach gender to the spiritual father-son relationship, we must deal with some very important questions: Who was the mother of Jesus? Who was the father of Jesus? Who was the mother of Christ? Who was the father of Christ? As we think in differentiating terms such as *Jesus* and *Christ*, it is imperative that we separate earthly from heavenly. Jesus is who made Christ legal in the earth in the same manner that "ish" made Adam legal in the earth. Likewise, your physical body is what makes you legal in the earth. If it was not for your physical body, you would not be legal in the earth, nor would you be able to remain in the earth.

When Jesus stepped down from his holy habitation to become the Word manifested in flesh, did He need a spiritual mother to make himself complete, or was He complete after He actually took his first step on his way to earth? The answer to both questions is, "Certainly not!" Jesus was already complete. His state of completeness was never contingent upon whether or not He had a spiritual mother. Jesus was and is complete in God. Let's prove this point by recalling to memory the question Jesus posed as recorded in the book of Luke: ***"How is it that ye sought me? wist ye not that I must be about my Father's business? (Luke 2:49).*** What father was Jesus talking about—his earthly or heavenly father? This question that

Jesus posed at the young age of twelve proves that He was, indeed, complete in God.

It must be understood that when God deals with sonship, he does not deal with gender. If we deal with the father-son relationship from an earthly perspective, we find the previously asked questions very difficult to answer as they pertain to this type of relationship. If we, however, deal with the father–son relationship from a heavenly perspective, we find God to be our ALL. The concept of the father-son relationship from a heavenly perspective shows us that fathering is not based upon gender, but upon the pattern of our heavenly father, who is and has become all to us.

Sonship, as we know it to be defined in the earth, requires both a mother and a father. This definition is supported by science, which teaches that the creation of a human requires an egg and a sperm. Biology professors have aptly taught us that life or conception necessitates the deposit and uniting of a man's sperm with a woman's egg. In simpler terms, children can be born only with the cooperation of two separate entities: a man and a woman. That's how children are formed; they receive their total genetic makeup from two separate contributions-one from the male (father) and one from the female (mother). Subsequently, it becomes commonplace for us to believe that every son— natural or spiritual—must have both a father and mother. This is, in a nutshell, an earthly perspective.

The heavenly perspective, or God's perspective, is vastly different. While it takes both father and mother in order to properly develop children in the natural, this is true only from an earthly perspective. In contrast, from the heavenly perspective, or God's perspective, God deposits **everything** you, as a son, need into your spiritual father. All that you need to become whom God created you to be is wrapped up on the inside of your spiritual father.

> *"For as many as are led by the Spirit of God, are the sons of God."* *Romans 8:14*

spiritual father. God's pattern of fathering does not require a spiritual mother.

The term "spiritual mother" has been used primarily because of our misunderstanding of the spiritual father concept and our enslavement to gender directives. When it comes to fathering, God is simply not concerned with gender. The Bible states the following:

If the Word of God is true, and it is, then being a spiritual *"son"* has nothing at all to do with gender. This clearly seen principle rings true not only for spiritual sons, but for spiritual fathers. Gender can't be attached to spiritual fathering in the earth.

> *"And God said, Let us make man in our image, after our likeness: and let them have dominion over the fish of the sea, and over the fowl of the air, and over the cattle, and over all the earth, and over every creeping thing that creepeth upon the earth."* *Genesis 1:26*

Therefore, the set gift or spiritual father may be male or female. However, if a pastor/set gift is a female, she may have biological children, but does not automatically become a spiritual mother to her biological children. Just as God has given to the male pastors/set gifts everything that their spiritual sons will need to reach their destiny, so he does with the female pastors/set gifts. "Female" is the package she comes in; "Father" is what is inside of the package.

What do you do with the birthing process if you are not going to deal with the father-son relationship from an earthly perspective? Dealing with the father-son relationship from an earthly perspective and excluding gender causes us to revisit the Genesis account.

The word "man" in this passage is derived from the Hebrew word "Adam" which is defined as "person" or "mankind." The word "Adam" can also refer to male or female (*The Hebrew Greek Study Bible*). In this writing, the term for man is referred to as one who was created, while the term "man" in Genesis 2:23, which is *"ish"—a masculine noun that distinguishes male from female*—refers to one who was made. Simply stated, we are discussing nothing less than the male, husband, mate, or male man. On the other hand, the word *"neqevah"* means *"woman or female whether human or animal."* The fact that this word is associated with the words "female," "woman," or "animal" confirms that it is an earthly term that answers to gender as opposed to a heavenly term that is not gender-specific and answers to God. If we choose to think in heavenly terms, we must drive out earthly terms.

"Heavenly" has no gender attached to it. "Earthly" has gender attached to it. If we look past gender, we will be able to see the father-son relationship as God sees it.

For example: this scripture makes reference to the heavenly or non-gender idea. It basically tells us that the son could be either male or female. Likewise, the father could be either male or female. Anytime you think that a father or a son could be male or female, you must realize that you are not dealing from an earthly perspective. In turn, if you are dealing with the thought that the gender makeup of a bride could either be male or female, you must—again—realize that you are not dealing from an earthly perspective. If we are dealing with *"ish"* (man) or *"neqevah"* (woman), then we are dealing from the earthly perspective and not the heavenly perspective.

> *"If ye then be risen with Christ, seek those things which are above, where Christ sitteth on the right hand of God. Set your affection on things above, not on things on the earth."*
> *Colossians 3:1-2*

> *"There is neither Jew nor Greek, there is neither bond nor free, there is neither male nor female: for ye are all one in Christ Jesus. And if ye be Christ's, then are ye Abraham's seed, and heirs according to the promise."*   *Galatians 3:28-29*

To aid us in our understanding of the father-son relationship, we must think in third-dimension terms as opposed to second-dimension terms. There are a lot of things that don't exist in the third dimension that we have grown accustomed to in the second dimension. When we begin to deal with earthly perspectives and groom ourselves to think solely in terms of earthly matters, God will admonish us as he did the Colossians.

This verse begins by saying *"if ye then be risen,"* indicating that it is possible that we could have a different concept or understanding than the author does. But if we are indeed risen, then we have to think on different terms. The terms that God suggests that we think on will require us to shift in our thinking and where we set our affections. Think on **things above**, and **set your affection on things above, not on things on the earth.**

Accomplishing this is going to call for a total transformation in our thought patterns. When we understand this, we will understand why we must embrace the father-son relationship from the heavenly perspective.

The Father–Son Relationship from a Heavenly Perspective

Many believers in the body of Christ are experiencing difficulties in embracing the father-son relationship. Much of the difficulty they experience is a direct result of the perspective they employ while considering the father-son relationship. The concept of the father-son relationship is not based upon an earthly understanding. If we try to exist in a spiritual father-son relationship based upon an earthly perspective, we will encounter an immeasurable amount of frustration and confusion. The father-son relationship, although it has been widely misunderstood within Christendom, originated from God and can be comprehended only by adopting a heavenly perspective.

Naturally, when we think of a "fathering" relationship, we automatically consider gender. "Only men can be fathers."

Well, this holds true in society, where there are gender boundaries, rightly set, in the earth. Because we are earthbound, when we think of fathering relationships, what generally come to mind is the many examples of fathers we have seen in the earth. However, when we regard a spiritual "fathering" relationship, the only example of a father that we need to look to is our heavenly father. Fortunately, God has established the heavenly pattern for the earthbound spiritual father to follow.

In order to understand the concept of the father-son relationship from a heavenly perspective, there are certain components that need to be in place so that this relationship can operate at its fullest potential, yielding benefits to both the father and the son.

The first component that we will examine in the father-son relationship is the *"teknon"* component.

The Teknon Component

In John 1, the apostle wrote: ***"But as many as received him, to them gave he power to become the sons [teknon] of God, even to them that believe on his name:"*** **(John 1:12)**. The Greek word for sons in this passage is "teknon." This word for son indicates that the person or persons spoken of are sons by birth. The teknon stage is the first stage, where a son actually reaches in the father-son relationship. It is a phase where, although he is a son, he has not reached full development. At this point, his features, although maturing, are not yet distinct. The "teknon" son may vaguely resemble the father; however, upon first glance, he is not immediately recognized as the son of his father. Further maturation and character development are needed. Yet, he is **still** a son.

The Huios Component

"Huios" is another Greek word for son and is used throughout the New Testament. This word is best exemplified when Paul exhorts the Corinthians to be followers of him. As a "huios," following or imitating, as another biblical version translates, is what the "huios" son does best. Unlike the "teknon" component of sonship, the "huios" component of sonship requires action. At the "huios" stage of sonship, the son displays marked and distinct features, revealing that he is indeed the son of his father. Unlike the "teknon" stage, this word for son indicates that the son is a son of character. "Elder, you act just like the pastor. You even say the same things he says. I'll tell you, if I weren't looking in your face I would've sworn that I had heard Bishop speaking." In the huios phase, the son takes on all of the characteristics of his father. He says what his father says, does what his father does, and acts as his father acts. Contrary to the "teknon" stage, this phase of sonship can be attained only by purposeful pursuit. The "huios" son is a son of purpose.

The Responsibility Component

Genesis 18, which details the patriarch Abraham and his angelic encounter, gives us a great outline of the responsibility component of sonship. Let us review some of the son's responsibilities, submission, obedience, and reciprocity:

Submission

> *"And he lift up his eyes and looked, and lo, three men stood by him: and when he saw them, he ran to meet them from the tent door, and bowed himself toward the ground."*
> Genesis 18:2

As Abraham bowed himself to the ground, he placed himself at the disposal of the angels, showing he had no defense. He was in a posture of total submission. In order to have a successful father–son relationship, the son must find himself revisiting the place of submission frequently.

Obedience

> *"And I will fetch a morsel of bread, and comfort ye your hearts; after that ye shall pass on: for therefore are you come to your servant. And they said, So do, as thou hast said. And Abraham hastened..."*
> Genesis 18:5-6

After declaring what he *would* do, the angels commanded him to do as he said. If you continue reading on, you will notice that Abraham **hastened.** Not only was Abraham obedient, he was quick to be obedient. Sons must hasten to be obedient. If you believe, as a son, that you must analyze and critique every command that your father gives, perhaps sonship and its fruit are not for you—and being an illegitimate son is.

Reciprocity

> *"And they said unto him, Where is Sarah thy wife? And he said, Behold, in the tent. And he said, I will certainly return unto thee according to the time of life; and lo, Sarah thy wife shall have a son..."*
> Genesis 18:9-10

How it is that reciprocity is considered to be a son's responsibility?

In the first eight verses of this chapter, Abraham is found serving to his heart's content. Abraham ran to meet the angels from the tent door, fetched their water, washed their feet, fetched them bread, and fetched a tender calf for them, and provided the angels with a tasty meal underneath the tree. What a servant! Now, Abraham's hour of reciprocity was nigh. It was his responsibility, in order to receive the reciprocal blessing, to be in place. As sons, each of our blessings has been addressed to our homes or dwelling places. Our homes, such as they are, have been addressed according to our lineage or line of succession. Your blessing will be sent only to the place that bears the name of your father. It is your responsibility to be at home and in place.

The Vulnerability Component

The son has the responsibility of willingly making himself vulnerable to his father. It is said of Timothy, ***"Him would Paul have to go forth with him; and took and circumcised him..."*** **(Acts 16:3).** Circumcision is the test of a true son. Successful circumcision requires total trust on the son's behalf. During this delicate procedure, the son must willingly bare all of his most private parts—to a man. He is not able to leave even the smallest portion of "his stuff" covered. All areas must be exposed to this man he calls his "spiritual father." In addition, the son must trust that his father has a steady and skillful hand as the procedure dictates. Should the son demonstrate even an iota of distrust, it is possible that what was intended to be a sign of covenant would result in an incidence of castration. Sons must allow themselves to trust their fathers, even to the point of self-exposure.

The Covenant Component

Covenant is one of the most sacred components in a relationship. It is what binds one person with another, one heart to another. Adam made an awesome pronouncement as he declared and ratified his covenantal relationship with his wife. Adam spoke these words regarding Eve: *"This is now bone of my bones, and flesh of my flesh:..."* **(Gen. 2:23).** The concept of a father–son relationship from a heavenly perspective calls for covenant. Believe it or not, we are recognized from heaven based upon our covenantal relationships. For example, after fleeing from the face of her mistress, Hagar is accosted by an angel of the Lord by the fountain in the way of Shur. The angel asks her, *"Hagar, Sarai's maid, whence camest thou?..."* **(Gen. 16:8)** Notice that he didn't address her as Hagar Smith, or Hagar, the girl from Kenilworth, but she was recognized from heaven by her covenantal relationship in the earth. This account accurately describes how sons are recognized in heaven—by their spiritual covenantal relationships in the earth. Without a daddy, you don't even have a name.

The Blessing Component

This component of the father-son relationship applies exclusively to the spiritual father. It is the responsibility of the father to bless the son, provided the son has done what is required of him to be blessed. When the father pronounces the blessing over the son, the words that he speaks sprout legs and arms. These words now become agents with the assignment to unlock every door and to release every promise into the hands of the son. The power these words possess to unlock doors and to release promises is not found solely in the words themselves, but in the position and authority of the father.

Impartation - Learning to Father Leaders

Before anyone can function as a father or a type of father, they must submit themselves under the hand of someone else on earth. There are times when the person to whom you need to submit may seem to be less capable than you, yet God still has you submit under their hand.

There was a time when Jesus, becoming ready for ministry, had one more person to whom He submitted to aside from the one that posed as His natural father (Joseph). The person to whom He submitted, after leaving Joseph, was John the Baptist at the baptism. John the Baptist felt very much incapable of baptizing Him, and He bears this out by saying, *"I have need to be baptized of thee"* (Matt. 3:14). That was the point when Jesus humbled Himself and submitted under the hand of John. He went from there to the wilderness to be tempted and to go through his period of being tried.

Jesus returned from the wilderness and began the selection of His sons for ministry. Yes, He himself hand-picked his own sons that he would pour into. The interesting thing about handpicking His own sons is that some had to leave their natural fathers and come under the authority of their spiritual father. Until we come under the authority of our spiritual father, we will never be able to function in the position as a son. There must be absolute submission under a father.

Let's look at some major details about their father-son relationship.

"Now when Jesus had heard that John was cast into prison, he departed into Galilee; And leaving Nazareth, he came and dwelt in Capernaum, which is upon the sea coast, in the borders of Zabulon and Nephthalim: That it might be fulfilled which was spoken by Esaias the prophet, saying, the land of Zabulon, and the land of Nephthalim, by the way of the sea, beyond Jordan, Galilee of the Gentiles; The people which sat in darkness saw great light; and to them which sat in the region and shadow of death light is sprung up. From that time Jesus began to preach, and to say, Repent: for the kingdom of heaven is at hand."   *Matthew 4:12-17*

"And Jesus, walking by the sea of Galilee, saw two brethren, Simon called Peter, and Andrew his brother, casting a net into the sea: for they were fishers. And he saith unto them, Follow me, and I will make you fishers of men. And they straightway left their nets, and followed him. And going on from thence, he saw other two brethren, James the son of Zebedee, and John his brother, in a ship with Zebedee their father, mending their nets; and he called them. And they immediately left the ship and their father, and followed him. And Jesus went about all Galilee, teaching in their synagogues and preaching the gospel of the kingdom, and healing all manner of sickness and all manner of disease among the people."
Matthew 4:18-23

---

1. Leaving Your Comfort Zone and Place of Support, v. 12

Jesus left the comfort of Nazareth, where He was raised, along with his family support and all that he cared about and loved. He came to a place that, later on, he would have to weep over because they hadn't grasped their time of visitation. This is a place where every father and every son have to meet. It's what I call a place of surrender and a place of abandonment. This place is a strange place where there is no moral support or spiritual support, only nothingness. This is that type of place that will cause many to wonder why you left and wonder what purpose could there possibly be for going to a place such as Capernaum. Every father must learn to exist where there is nothing but surrender. Every son must come to a place with a father where there is nothing to do but surrender and sit at his feet. There is great power at the feet of a master teacher for the son if he only learns to wait.

2. Shining for or in another Man's Dream, v. 16

Jesus, at this point, realizes that his only position is to shine for another man's purpose. As a son, it is imperative that we understand that unless we shine for another man's dream, we'll never see the fulfillment of our own dreams. As we understand this very important position, we'll also understand the way to fatherhood. The ultimate is to become a father and not remain only a son. We find later that the disciples (sons) were called by Jesus (father) to shine in his dream, which was to reach the lost at all cost. My question to you is: "Are you trying to shine for yourself when you have been called into another man's dream?" If you are, your dream can never be realized because you are trying to shine in your dream when yours has never died.

3. Preaching another Man's Word, v. 17

It is amazing to me that Jesus came preaching the same Word that John the Baptist preached. Remember that Jesus submitted himself under the hand of John the Baptist and never showed himself until John the Baptist was going off the scene. A son can never show himself until the father is going off the scene. There is a problem in our society today. We, as sons, are trying to show ourselves before our father has gone off the scene. John the Baptist, being a type of a father in this case, was not dead, but just off the scene. It is not necessary for your father to be dead, but it is necessary for him to be off the scene. Note also that it is important to always stay in a submitted position under your father until he comes to a place of nonexistence. This marks the time for your arising. The real test of whether your time has come is how well you speak your father's word. There will always be an increase of knowledge and revelation that may supersede what your father has said, but it is only likely to happen after he ceases to exist. His death becomes your rising.

4. Locating Your Sons, vv. 18-19

At this point, Jesus starts the process of locating his sons, who will function as his staff. God always causes a father to locate sons, or staff. Not only does God cause a father to locate his sons, but he also causes him to place his spirit on his sons in order to reproduce what he has been made as a father. There is a word that comes to mind when I, as a father, think of a son or daughter. I have the awesome challenge to duplicate myself in them and to say what Jesus said, *"Follow me, and I will make you fishers of men."* The condition of a son is to "follow me." Any son who has a problem following the father (leader) forfeits the benefit of having a portion of that father. The word "follow" is extremely important to having a portion of your father's spirit. This means you must follow at all cost. Sometimes the cost is great and sometimes not so great. At any rate, there is a cost to capturing the spirit of your father.

The benefit of following is "I will make you." The making comes during the process of following. The word "following" is progressive, is continuous, and illustrates a method of not stopping the said action. The making happens as you continue following. Some have forfeited their making because they ceased in their following. Now, we return to the prerequisite, *"Follow me, and I will make you fishers of men."*

I will make you that which I am. God told Moses to choose seventy elders who were faithful, of a good report, and full of wisdom. Although the elders (sons) had those qualities, God still said there was yet something lacking. They had great gifting and great qualities, yet the missing ingredient to activate all of that greatness was the spirit of their father. God said to Moses, "You choose the men and I will take of the spirit upon thee and will put it upon them." (Num. 11:16-17) The spirit that God was referring to within the context of this scripture would be equivalent to the anointing that was smeared upon Moses.

5. Leaving the Natural Father and Cleaving to the Spiritual Father, v. 20

It was a custom for the natural father to teach natural hobbies and abilities. The spiritual father was the one who had the challenge to impart spiritual gifts.

The Purpose of the 21st Century Prophet

The prophet is multifaceted in both operation and assignment. If the prophet does not remain and operate within his particular assignment, or sphere where he dominates he will waiver and never fulfill his purpose. What is the prophet's assignment? The prophet's assignment is:

To Locate Lost Children

"Behold, I will send you Elijah the prophet before the coming of the great and dreadful day of the Lord: And he shall turn the heart of the fathers to the children, and the heart of the children to their fathers, lest I come and smite the earth with a curse."   *Malachi 4:5-6*

It is important to note that we, as prophets—even Senior Prophets—have the assignment of locating lost children. In this hour when God is revealing or exposing bastards, it is imperative that the prophet locate lost children so that the children's hearts can be turned to their fathers and so that the curse can be eliminated.

In addition, prophets must be mindful to turn the hearts of the children to **their** fathers. We must not overlook the possessive pronoun "their." Prophets should never desire someone else's children but should always send the children back to **their** fathers.

We (as set gifts) often make the mistake of calling ourselves someone's father simply because they are our members. This is not always the case. Just because they are members does not make them children, nor does it make us fathers. We may **not** be their fathers. In fact, we may only be *"instructors"* to them (1 Cor. 4:15). Once we understand where we are, we must begin the process of turning the children's hearts back to **their** fathers.

NOTE

CHAPTER
3

Developing from the Bedchamber

There is an assault on the anointing on the body of Christ and we must protect it with everything that we have. We as men and women of God should rise up with the pureness of God coming out of our heart, so that everything that we say surely comes to pass. We have to become a prophetic voice in the area where we live. People should be looking for a word from God from your mouth. They should be able to say there is a man of God or a woman of God in this city.

There is an anointing that rest on us to do what God has assigned to us in a particular season. But some of us have walked in our own ways, and have not understood that there is an anointing that is on us. The mindset of some of us question why God would want to use us and we have let the anointing that is on our lives lie dormant.

Anointed for a Reason and a Season

There is an anointing on you and in you for a specific reason. It is in you so that you will be able to come to the highest height in God that your flesh will allow. Most people within the body of Christ never reach the height of their anointing, because their flesh has prevented them from doing so. Then there is an anointing that is upon you and that anointing shifts. That anointing is on one assignment in this season, but it shifts to another assignment in the next season. The anointing on you is specifically tailored to your assignment. There is a link between what your assignment is and the anointing that rests on you. We must understand what is on us in a particular season and why it is there.

The anointing is not just on your pastor or set gift. It is not just on your man or woman of God. If you get close enough to him or her, that same anointing rolls down on you. You cannot go into a room where there is an aroma, and that aroma does not get on you. No matter how much perfume or cologne you put on in the morning; when you walk into a 7-Eleven about 7AM, there is an aroma of coffee that will be on you when you leave out of the store; even if you have not gone near the coffee. If a natural product like coffee can linger on you, then if you stay under your man or woman of God, the anointing on them comes down on you. The ultimate anointing that you are experiencing actually rest on your man or woman of God. He or she has an anointing to preach, to teach, to usher, to sing, to play music, to clean the floor, to wash walls, to clean toilets, to change light bulbs, to produce books, etc. They have an anointing to do everything in the church that needs to be done. But since he or she cannot not do all of that, and still do what God told them to do, they passed that anointing off on you.

Understand that the anointing is on us to bring change. People assemble themselves around you because of the anointing. They see something on you that you are not conscious of – the anointing. Jesus talks about this in Luke 4:18:

> *"The Spirit of the Lord is upon me, because he hath anointed me to preach the gospel to the poor; he hath sent me to heal the brokenhearted, to preach deliverance to the captives, and recovering of sight to the blind, to set at liberty them that are bruised," Luke 4:18*

This is the reason that the poor, the brokenhearted, the sick, those that are burdened, those that have a need and those that are pushed to the side come around. These kinds of folks come around you all of the time, because you have an anointing on your life.

What is the Anointing?

The anointing that rest upon us is on us for a particular reason, there is something specifically that you are called to do. *According to Isaiah 10:27, "And it shall come to pass in that day, that his burden shall be taken away from off thy shoulder, and his yoke from off thy neck, and the yoke shall be destroyed because of the anointing."* The anointing is something that will destroy yokes and lifts every heaven burdens. So when you and I are carrying out a particular assignment that we think is too heavy, the anointing rest on you in order to make that assignment light. The anointing is classified as your unction to function. We find that in *1 John 2:20 "But ye have an unction from the Holy One, and ye know all things."* You and I have a particular assignment and in order to function in that assignment we need an anointing.

We have an anointing to function. The anointing that rests on you enables you to do what you thought you could not do. There is a level of trouble that comes to us in order to flush us out of a comfort zone. Whenever you are in the wrong spot, your anointing does not work. When God is able to push you out of the place where you seem to be comfortable, it is at that point that the anointing is able to work, because the whole focus of where you live, inside looks like you are going to sink. Our anointing works under pressure and that is the best place for it to work. Anytime we are under pressure our anointing can work there. Remember it is not a matter of your ability, but the ability of the anointing that rests on your life. When you begin to place all of the emphasis on the anointing that rests on you and not your ability, you begin to flow. Until you become conscious of the anointing that rests on you, you will never get a flow to preach, teach or whatever you are assigned to do. For example, musicians that flow in the anointing, recognize that it is not just going to be about playing written or practiced notes, but there is going to be a sound you hear that is not on the paper. Or when you are preaching the gospel, you will hear and say something that is not on the page or in your notes.

The Cost of the Anointing

However, the anointing comes at a cost. You must pay for it. Most of us are not really willing to pay for the anointing that is on us, because our life is not our own. You cannot go where you want to go; you cannot do what you want to do; or pursue what you think you need to be pursuing. You have to analyze and evaluate people who come into your space, by asking yourself if they are capable of going where I go. This is a concern because not all of us understand where we are going, nor have we really understood the trouble that comes into our lives.

We think that the things that have befallen us are just normal things. The enemy cannot see what is in you, but he can see what is on you. When he gets a whiff of what is on your life, he comes after it. Athaliah is coming after your anointing because without it, you are nothing more than a religious person. Her name was called Athaliah, but the spirit of Athaliah is an anointing killer. Athaliah became queen after her mother Jezebel. Ahab was her father. Once her son died, her objective was to make sure that she was in power.

Now we have an interesting situation of Athaliah, the anointing killer, being the daughter of Jezebel, the Prophet killer. Jezebel was the one who paralyzed Israel with idol worship and now that she had Israel dysfunctional, she raises up her daughter in order to paralyze Judah. Knowing that Judah is symbolic of praise causes us to realize that we need an anointing to rise up. One of the things that a lot of us do, is hinder the anointing that is designed to bring forth the thing, that is designed to set us free.

A woman does not have a Jezebel spirit because she wears makeup. This is a camouflage to get the church, which is a voice in front of the people, off, by thinking that the spirit of Jezebel has to do with makeup; so that you do not identify it when Jezebel really comes after you. The spirit of Jezebel still lives and it is an anointing killer. Her name changed to Athaliah. Athaliah was coming after all of the king's seed, the seed royal.

Identifying Athaliah

Let's take a look at 2 Kings 11:1-3:

"And when Athaliah the mother of Ahaziah saw that her son was dead, she arose and destroyed all the seed royal. 2 But Jehosheba, the daughter of king Joram, sister of Ahaziah, took Joash the son of Ahaziah and stole him from among the king's sons which were slain; and they hid him, even him and his nurse, in the bedchamber from Athaliah, so that he was not slain. 3 And he was with her hid in the house of the LORD six years. And Athaliah did reign over the land."

The spirit of Jezebel will go after that which the anointing is passed on to. One way to identify it is that it is perverted. It takes a certain kind of a perversion for a grandmother to kill her own seed, in order to take office herself. She was killing all of her son's children so that they would not come into power and she would reign. But Ahaziah's sister took the youngest, Joash, and took him into the bedchamber of the Lord and hid him for six years. Even though Joash was a baby at that particular time, there was an anointing on him. The objective was to guard the anointing on Joash, because he was the king. There was an anointing in him and on him because he was to step into the office to carry out a particular assignment.

This was the first time a woman ever stepped into office as a Queen and it was because she wiped out all of the king's sons. She wipes out all of the authority. The spirit of Jezebel goes after the authority. God has already ordained and set you aside for a very specific reason - so that you would step into power. Now the job of Athaliah is to make sure that you who are supposed to step into power never get at the gate of power. We must protect what is in us and on us.

Now there are a lot of us that are power seekers. We want to be great, rather than just operating on the anointing that lives in us. We want to rush this thing; we want to become somebody. We want to get in front of somebody, but God says just stay with the anointing that is on you. Do not seek opportunity or fame; just stay with the anointing that is on you. The fact that you and I may be chasing fame down means that we are already following Athaliah and it is set out to kill the anointing that is on us.

She was not interested in the house of the Lord. When it comes down to that spirit, there is a disinterest in authority. We will hide from authority. When God sets up spiritual authority, it is for our protection. Spiritual authority will take us into the bedchamber. I have been watching this because some of us look like spiritual whores or prostitutes (male or female) and not a wife. Athaliah is a whore spirit; it is a spirit of prostitution and it does not want to make a commitment. But when it comes down to being a wife, she has signed on the dotted line saying I am with you for the rest of my time; I am committed to you, and I am submitted to you. You are my man and I am your wife. This is covenant and commitment. Have you ever heard someone say that they are only at a particular church for a season? That is the spirit of Athaliah. You should be committed to whatever you marry. Whenever you come into a covenant with something, you should be committed.

Athaliah realizes that she cannot send you back into your mother's womb, she cannot stop the words that come out of your mouth, she cannot stop who you are, she cannot do any of those things, so she comes in unawares. She does exactly what Jude said, she creeps into the church unaware.

"For there are certain men crept in unawares, who were before of old ordained to this condemnation, ungodly men, turning the grace of our God into lasciviousness, and denying the only Lord God, and our Lord Jesus Christ." Jude 4

Athaliah comes as if she is pushing you forth.

You must have a revelation of who you are with. This is true of every relationship in your life, because if Jude is correct and he is, they can creep in unaware. They cannot do anything about who you are, nor can they do anything about God's call on your life; but they can shut down your anointing.

Peter addresses that with Sapphira in Acts 5:9:

"Then Peter said unto her, How is it that ye have agreed together to tempt the Spirit of the Lord? behold, the feet of them which have buried thy husband are at the door, and shall carry thee out." Acts 5:9

Peter wanted to know why Sapphira chose to agree with her lawless husband. Peter is suggesting that she has a God-given right not to agree with her husband, but she chose to agree with his lawlessness. Her agreement with him is now costing her life.

Then fell she down straightway at his feet, and yielded up the ghost: and the young men came in, and found her dead, and, carrying her forth, buried her by her husband.   Acts 5:10

One cannot use submission as an excuse to be lawless.

Remember, the spirit of Althaliah is not clearly seen. The spirit of Athaliah can only be traced by what it does. Let's say for instance if you are a woman and you are in relationship with a man, if he is the reason for you now shutting down all or some given assignments that your man or woman of God has given you, it might be traced to or aligned with the spirit of Athaliah. Remember, her purpose is to shut down the anointing.

Hidden in the Bedchamber

Now remember verse 2:

"But Jehosheba, the daughter of king Joram, sister of Ahaziah, took Joash the son of Ahaziah and stole him from among the king's sons which were slain; and they hid him, even him and his nurse, in the bedchamber from Athaliah, so that he was not slain."

Jehosheba was in the same linage as Athaliah. They came from the same root, yet she was the one that saved the king who was only a year old. Remember we said before that Athaliah killed all of her grandchildren, so that she could be the first one that rises up as queen of Judah. She would be calling all of the shots and would be the one to lead the entire nation of Judah; she killed all of the royal seed.

Athaliah would have killed baby Joash knowing that the baby had right to the throne. But Jehosheba stole Joash and took him into the bedchamber to make sure that the stuff that was on him was protected. The anointing was not on him at the time, because it was not time for him to be recognized as king, but he was the anointed of God on the inside, because of who God called him to be.

Some of you are not where you belong because you are stolen so that the anointing on you would be protected. God knows what you are to become. He has put something on the inside of you, and He is not going to let a whore get to you. God is not going to let anything take you down. So He had you stolen from where you were and hidden in the house. Now if we are not careful, after having escaped the spirit of Athaliah, we may prematurely run out of the bedchamber with the Lord; and she will see us and recognize that we are the anointed of the Lord, and get her next opportunity to kill us.

There is an anointing in you and there is anointing on you. When the anointing comes on you, it comes on you because you are ready for service. When you were born, there was an anointing within, because God had already called you and named you prophet, but you were not ready for service, so no anointing could come on you. When the anointing comes on you, the devil has a right to attack you. Joash was in the middle of all of this, but Jehosheba grabs him, steals him from the rest of the children, hides him in the bedchamber and he stays in the bedchamber for six years. Six is symbolic of creation and whatever God wants to create on the inside of us may take six years or it may even take sixty years, but you have to stay hidden in the house until it is time to go forth.

The enemy comes after you because of the anointing that is on you, and Athaliah wants to kill the anointing that is on you. When you and I run all over the place, run where we want to go, do what we want to do, we are opening ourselves up to the spirit of Athaliah. If you come out before time, Athaliah will see you and kill you before you come into what you are designed to do.

Who is trying to hide you?

Remember, Athaliah is not a female. The old church school wants us to believe that Jezebel was a woman with makeup and earrings. That within itself was a motivation by the spirit of Athaliah, to get the whole religious community off course of what it really was. We are thinking of a Jezebel spirit as someone with makeup and earrings, and that takes our mind completely off of the real spirit of Athaliah. Remember how God used Jehosheba to hide Joash? God also used Rehab in Josh 2:4-6:

"And the woman took the two men, and hid them, and said thus, There came men unto me, but I wist not whence they were: 5 And it came to pass about the time of shutting of the gate, when it was dark, that the men went out: whither the men went I wot not: pursue after them quickly; for ye shall overtake them. 6 But she had brought them up to the roof of the house, and hid them with the stalks of flax, which she had laid in order upon the roof."

God used a prostitute to hide his anointed. Who keeps hiding you so that the anointing killer cannot get to you? Who keeps hiding you so that you are not seen so that the devil cannot kill you?

Samson had a Delilah, a heathen wife. That was his Athaliah. His parents were the ones that tried to hide him by telling him to stay away from the heathen women. We see this in Judges 14:3:

"Then his father and his mother said unto him, Is there never a woman among the daughters of thy brethren, or among all my people, that thou goest to take a wife of the uncircumcised Philistines? And Samson said unto his father, Get her for me; for she pleaseth me well."   Judges 14:3

He said "she pleases me well." That says that he was more connected with his flesh and his imprisoned soul, than he was connected with his spirit, who was in fellowship with God, to bring his imprisoned soul to holiness.

The Importance of a Covering

Now all Joash had to do was to stay under his covering and be hidden in the house, and Athaliah would not have seen him. That is all you have to do is stay hidden in the house. If you stay hidden behind your man or woman of God, you will be alright. We are not standing in the church we are set in the church. According to 1 Cor 12:28:

"And God hath set some in the church, first apostles, secondarily prophets, thirdly teachers, after that miracles, then gifts of healings, helps, governments, diversities of tongues." *1 Corinthians 12:28*

God has set us where we belong and we are to stay hidden under our covering until it is time to be exposed.

To get away from Athaliah, you must get in the bedchamber and stay covered by your man or woman of God - your God-given authority. There is only one head in the church. Remember the seeing, hearing and speaking are in the head and the working is in the body. We need our head to tell the rest of our body what to do. We need to stay hidden behind and under our authority until it is time to go out. There are times it seems so hard to stay under authority, because it seems like authority wants to hurt us. But God has set us under authority for our protection.

You do make room for yourself to come out. The bible says in *Prov 18:16 "A man's gift maketh room for him, and bringeth him before great men."* Your gift makes room for you. Remember there's an anointing on your life and if the Devil ever gets a glimpse of your anointing, he will send an Athaliah after you to make sure that you make all of the wrong decisions. Remember, Joash was hidden for six years and in the seventh year he was sent forth. At seven years old, Athaliah sees the king's son and realizes that her government has been overthrown. Athaliah cried, "Treason, treason," in other words you have deceived me.

Not just anybody can expose you. You have to be exposed by your covering. You have to give up your will in this area. Joash did not have a will. He was stolen against his will, he was hidden against his will and brought into the bedchamber, where he could not be attacked by Athaliah; and he stayed covered until it was time to come out. Your covering must be one that does not tolerate rebellion, because it is at the root of Athaliah; not only rebellion, but corruption and perversion also lives in her roots.

The Affects of Athaliah

Once Athaliah is allowed to get her hook into you, your spirit starts to change. Remember what Jesus said in Luke 4:18-21: *"The Spirit of the Lord is upon me, because he hath anointed me to preach the gospel to the poor; he hath sent me to heal the brokenhearted, to preach deliverance to the captives, and recovering of sight to the blind, to set at liberty them that are bruised, 19 To preach the acceptable year of the Lord. 20 And he closed the book, and he gave it again to the minister, and sat down. And the eyes of all them that were in the synagogue were fastened on him. 21 And he began to say unto them, This day is this scripture fulfilled in your ears."* Jesus went through all that He was assigned to do and when He began to say something, they would not let Him finish talking. *Luke 4:22 "and they said, Is not this Joseph's son?* They wanted to kill His anointing. When His anointing was seen, the spirit of Athaliah wanted to kill it. Remember when your anointing is seen, Athaliah comes after it to kill it.

I am not talking about someone that is opposed to or jealous of your anointing, but someone that has already launched a plan to assassinate it; someone that rises up to make sure that you are out there and exposed when it is not time, because you still need to be in the bedchamber. I am not talking about someone that wants to keep you in a place of safety. Understand this; there is safety in the bedchamber. If I am having a challenge in my prayer life, it means that Athaliah is trying to pull me out of the bedchamber, because my bedchamber is where I am praying and am intimate with God. Remember, your wife is in the bedchamber. We are married to God and there is safety in His bedchamber. We become intimate with Him in the bedchamber. You never take a whore into the bedchamber.

Another thing about a wife, you do not keep secrets from her. When you are intimate with your wife, you do not keep secrets from your her. Another way to identify Athaliah is that she wants you to keep secrets from the father or who God has actually set over your life that is designed to protect you. I am leery of people who want you to keep secrets because it is the mark of the spirit of Athaliah. Athaliah wants to become intimate with you and then does not want you to tell anybody.

Samson, as powerful as he was fell to the spirit of Athaliah. He trusted Delilah in spite of the number of times she set him up. You have to check out those you trust. How do you trust a man or a woman that keeps setting you up? Once you yield to the spirit of Athaliah, you don't recognize a set up. You have been overtaken by that lying spirit and are fooled by it. Samson's parents tried to protect him by telling him not to go after those heathen women; but because Athaliah was already at work, he did not pay attention to his authority.

Have you ever known that something was taking you down and you kept on doing it anyway? Your flesh was submitted to the spirit of Athaliah. Your soul (mind, will and intellect) says what Sampson said "she please me well." The spirit of Athaliah gets you to a place where you no longer listen to reason.

In addition to that, Elijah had a Jezebel, which is where that spirit of Athaliah came from and he had that same challenge. He still had a lot of good years left; Athaliah sold him on a lie, and said that "all the prophets are dead." The minute we start putting our attention on everybody else or what everybody else is doing, then we have began to be influenced by the spirit of Athaliah. Remember we talked about Ananias and his wife Sapphira; they sold a piece of property and lied to the Holy Spirit. Sapphira was overtaken by the spirit of Athaliah, because she agreed with her lying husband who was submitted to the spirit of Athaliah. You cannot be overtaken by Athaliah unless you agree.

The Process of Being Hidden

You have to stay hidden in the house until it is time for your anointing to be exposed. The reason you are hidden in the house is so that your anointing would grow strong so that by the time your anointing is six years old, you are ready to be exposed. Joash was hidden in the house for six years. He was seven years old when he was crowned king. He was not crowned until he was complete. It is not time to come out of the house, until you are complete. The bedchamber is the place where God hides you, feeds you, teaches you doctrine and how to pray.

When you come out of the bedchamber, you know how to submit to authority. It is the place where you learn submission. In the bedchamber, you lose all issues and learn the proper attitude. The bedchamber is where all deals are settled.

There is an anointing that is on your life, even if it does not seem like it. In the bedchamber is where we get that anointing developed. In the bedchamber we can prophecy and be wrong, and no one will call you a false prophet. We can get corrected in the bedchamber as long as we are submitted under authority. We can get cleaned up in the bedchamber. Joash was hidden in the bedchamber. He was hidden in the house of the Lord. Athaliah did not go anywhere near the house of the Lord.

NOTE

SEASON #3
SEASON OF MATURITY

ma|tu|rity

n. ME *maturite* < L *maturitas*
1. the state or quality of being mature; specif., *a*) a being full-grown, ripe, or fully developed *b*) a being perfect, complete, or ready

2. *a*) a becoming due *b*) the time at which a note, etc. becomes due

--taken from *Webster's New World Dictionary*

The season of maturity is the season when God starts to work on your coming into who you are in God. I understand you know that you are called. You also know that you are anointed by now; that is normally your persuasion. The thing that is not clear is, what type of a prophet am I? In this season you don't only need to know that you are called, you need to know to what area you are called. What problem are you called to solve? Through this time where God is maturing you, your realm of authority will be realized.

The type of prophet you are will speak loudly in this season. There will be things that will be manifested in this season that have not been manifested prior to this time. You will identify your state or quality of being mature. I know your price is far above rubies, but how far above rubies? What exactly are you worth in the earth?

Your worth has to be valued according to your level of development and maturity. Those who have great ability to solve great problems are the ones that are paid great. If you solve great problems, then you are worth much. You can determine your worth on your job according to what they are willing to pay you. The level to which you have been developed and matured has been measured by what your job is willing to pay you. No one likes to hire people who bring problems, but everyone loves to hire those who solve problems.

In this season you state your worth. How do you state your worth? You state it by your commitment to maturity and development. Paul said, *"But I keep under my body, and bring it into subjection: lest that by any means, when I have preached to others, I myself should be a castaway."* (1 Cor. 9:27)

Let this be a time when you will beat your body and make it your slave so that you are not disqualified for the prize. Commit to maturity and development.

CHAPTER 4

Prophetic Faith Concepts

I t is important to understand the types of faith concepts that directly affect the prophet's office. There may be more, but these are the ones we will deal with.

- Giving as a principle,
- Receiving,
- Declaring against all odds,
- Decreeing a thing,
- Functioning where you have no points of reference and lastly,
- Calling those things that are not as though they are.

Three Types of Giving

Many Prophets desire to walk in all of the blessings of God yet they have not understood how to tap into that place which unlocks abundance. Most of us as prophets don't function in giving ourselves as a principle. We want others to do what we don't do by principle. Giving is one of those areas that we don't practice what we preach. God dealt with me at one point as I sought to understand wealth principles. I was one that tithed and gave offerings as I was able to do so.

Then one day I came to understand three powerful principles that set me free financially. And my assignment is to teach it to those that desire to come out of financial bondages and break through the financial barriers they are in. And yes there is an anointing on this giving message! The anointing being, that which destroys bondages. If it did not break or destroy a yoke or bondage it was not anointed.

Systematic Giving

This is when you give by a system that is already established or will be. Tithing is God's system for security and blessing. You have to cooperate with the system by tithing and giving offerings.

This giving plan is found over in the book of Malachi 3:10:

> *"Bring ye all the tithe into the storehouse, that there may be meat in mine house, and prove me now herewith, saith the Lord of hosts"*... *Malachi 3:10*

When anyone systematically participates God will automatically do several things:

a. Open the windows of heaven,
b. Pour out a blessing too large to receive at one time,
c. Will rebuke the devourer for you, and

d. Bring your harvest in its time.

God said He would do all of these things because of what we do systematically with the tithe and offerings. We must understand that this must be done on a regular consistent basis. Systematic giving is like an insurance plan, as long as you pay your premium, you and all your stuff are covered. When your payments go lacking, the policy is in default and there are consequences.

Spontaneous Giving

This form of giving occurs when there is an unexpected request made. There are times that we come to a point in our life where God is asking for something from us we had not planned for. You have to understand this is what makes it spontaneous giving. Now this kind of giving accesses something in the earth realm that is over and above the regular yet not "Supernatural." Luke 6:38 says: ***"Give and it shall be given unto you; good measure, pressed down, and shaken together, and running over, shall men give into your bosom."*** This is not accessing the supernatural realm in your giving though this is nice. Men at this point of giving are charged to start looking for you to give to you. Spontaneous giving always will attract mankind to give to you. This is a law that we have tapped into and many don't understand how this law works. So when the opportunity presents itself many don't move on it. What is the difference then between systematic giving and spontaneous giving? The difference is systematic giving is your managing what belongs to God and therefore God rewards your faithfulness. Whereas spontaneous giving is your giving out of what you don't have to give. However you are participating in an investment opportunity that causes men to be driven to give to you.

Sacrificial Giving

Now this is the type of giving that access the supernatural realm in its return. We see this giving plan operating many times in the Bible. In **1Kings 17** the widow woman was selected by God to provide for Elijah yet her position was not conducive for that kind of situation. Think about who she had to take care of: Elijah, the baby, herself and her household. What made it supernatural? The return coming instantly and over time made it supernatural. What made it a sacrifice? Because it was all she had and it was to go to her man of God as a first fruit made it a sacrifice. By principle God does not glory in someone's last, but does glory in someone's first. Now this is why most people don't come into a supernatural harvest: either do they give their last, or maybe their man of God does not permit them. This is the breaker on both sides. The man of God suffers by seeing you give your last and don't want to receive it, or you want to hold on to your last. This is a principle that I worked to increase in my life when I was working for almost nothing.

Examples of Sacrificial Giving:

* The lad with the fish and the loaves
* The widow with the cruise of oil

2 Corinthians 9:6-8 set the stage for our understanding the giving process and under what plan we desire to enter. The

choice has always been ours. We have said, "When God wants to bless us, He will" however nothing could be further from the truth. God has always put our financial future in our hands. We have just either out of ignorance or out of an unwilling heart decided we were not going to cooperate with the giving plan. 2 Corinthians 9:6-8 in the Amplified Bible says:

"Remember this: he who sows sparingly and grudgingly will also reap sparingly and grudgingly, and he who sows generously that blessings may come to someone will also reap generously and with blessings. Let each one give as he has made up his own mind and purposed in his heart, not reluctantly or sorrowfully or under compulsion for God loves (he takes pleasure in, prizes above other things, and is unwilling to abandon or to do without, a cheerful (joyous, prompt to do it) giver whose heart is in his giving. And God is able to make all grace (every favor and earthly blessing) come in abundance, so that you may always and under all circumstances and whatever the need be self sufficient [possessing enough to require no aid or support and furnished in abundance for every good work and charitable donation]."   *2 Corinthians 9:6-8 AMP*

– PROPHETIC EXCHANGE –

Philippians 4:10 describes the Prophetic Exchange. Prophetic Exchange is when you let those who are over your life spiritually (pastor, mentor or covering) receive of your natural things so that you can receive of their spiritual things (anointing, gifts, grace and oil).

When I sensed the level of revelation that was on some of those that I was tapped into in the various seasons of my growth, I made sure there was a Prophetic Exchange that took place. What that means is, I give to them of my natural things (treasure, time and/or talent) and I have a right to receive from them (anointing, oil, gifts, grace and favor). I have a right to receive from you if I sow into you. What is it that we receive? What is it that Paul received? Paul received relief, financial relief, from the church of Philippi and often times he received of their time. They then had a right to the grace that was on his life, to walk in his grace and favor.

Jesus said, "My grace is sufficient for thee; My strength is made perfect in weakness." We want to grab hold of that, but He was not talking to us. He was talking to Paul, because Paul had matured to a particular level. And Jesus said, "No, Paul, I am not going to do this for you. You do this for you." And He said, "My grace, Paul, is sufficient for thee." He was really teaching Paul: "Those that are coming up in ranks behind you, Paul, those that you are pouring into, wait until you see that they have matured to a certain level, and then say, 'My grace that's on me, which is the grace that Jesus put on me, is sufficient for you.'" So that is a Prophetic Exchange.

You can't buy it; it is not for sale. It is a reciprocal system: when you give of your natural things, it is an exchange that comes back to you in a prophetic release, or the things that you need in your spiritual life.

So Paul declares particular things, he says you have passageway now. You can enter in; it is your choice. I want to urge you that all God has prepared, you and I can enter into, but we have to want this.

I will never forget when I was at Jericho; Apostle Betty whom we affectionately know as Mom Betty, did not know that I had said this. Out of a thousand or so people, I watched her and Bishop Peebles, and I said I want that, that supernatural ability that they have and the level of revelation, I want that. Whatever it takes, I want it. Whatever they know, I want that. Every book that they talked about, I purchased. Every Bible that they mentioned, I purchased. I had to believe the money in because I had to have that. I would not leave out of there without purchasing a tape. I wanted what was on them. I had to know it. I made a sacrifice. I gave up all those pleasures and pastimes, "I gave it all up, God, and I want that. I need this." God said, "Rodney, Prophetic Exchange. What do you give? What are you going to give?" I will make every possible sacrifice, because I do want it. Money is not dear to me; I want that. What will you give for that which you desire to tap into? "I sell out to you, God." I have to have that costly anointing.

Just the normal church life was not good enough for me. You have to get to the place where the normal church life is not good enough for you. Just to walk as a mere human that has gone through church, that's not good enough. I'm selling out to you right now, Father. I sell out to You. This, I have to have: divine ability to do anything. I need divine ability to tap in there.

I watched this anointing on two people. Bishop Peebles would run by people, and healing and deliverances would take place, just because he ran by. "God, I want that." "Rodney, are you willing to pay the price?"

Everything else is secondary. You have to make God your choice. You have to decide to put sin down, and make God your choice.

There is a tremendous cost. Are you willing to pay that cost? Just the norm is not good enough. I have to have more. I need manifestation.

God spoke to me: "Rodney, if you want all that you say you want, sell out to Me." "What do you mean, sell out?" "Give it all up. Rodney work for Me. That means you have to give Me your will. That means when you want to, and I don't want you to, you can't." I had to fight "me" on occasion. I decided, God, I want all of you. I want to receive it. And I realize it comes through Prophetic Exchange.

God, if you give me the anointing, I can do this. The anointing answers all. What is it that you feel like you can't do? Receive the anointing. Receive the anointing. Sell out to God. It doesn't matter where you are right now, sell out to God.

NOTE

SEASON #4
SEASON OF EQUIPPING

equip

vt. **equipped, equipping** [Fr. e*quiper* < OFr *esquiper*, to embark, put out to sea, prob. < ON *skipa*, to arrange, make ready < *skip*

1. to provide with what is needed; outfit [troops *equipped* for battle]

2. to prepare by training, instruction, etc.

3. to dress (oneself) for a certain purpose

—*SYN* FURNISH
equip
abbrev. equipment

—taken from *Webster's New World Dictionary*

In the season of equipping we will find that the pressure will be on an increase. Pressure is something that either pushes you back or will cause you to go beyond the pressure to victory. The season of equipping pushes you to make decisions. We often times don't like to make final decisions on things, particularly as it pertains to relationships, or things we have to overcome. As you go through this season you will find that circumstances starts to push you as an indication that you must decide. You have to decide to grow, mature, and to finish. This is the season that could very well make the difference between your going forward or your quitting and never returning again.

What price are you willing to pay to grow in the things of God? To grow in the things of God, you have to start out with a made up mind. There are all kinds of things that will attack your growth. If you have a made up mind, you will not let anything stop you short of what you are after in God. Luke 18:1 says, *"And he spake a parable unto them to this end, that men ought always to pray, and not to faint."* The Amplified Bible says, *"...they ought always to pray and not to turn coward (faint, lose heart, and give up)."* Remember that God gives anointing only to those who have staying power. If we are going to be all that God is saying, we will have qualified for the equipping of and the equipment that comes along with that season. What are you willing to pay in order for that to happen? God will match your standing with the anointing for that season and the seasons to come.

If you are willing, God will give you everything necessary for you to be victorious in whatever your challenge is. Remember, this season is only to equip you for victory. The test that comes in this season is not to kill you. All that Peter, James and John went through was not designed to kill them. What kills us in the season of equipping is failing to finish. When we fail to finish, we open the door to many other things. There is a price to be paid, so think like a soldier.

CHAPTER 5

The Message of the Prophet

In many cases, prophetic people receive a word that is for an individual, not for the entire church. Therefore, it is important to understand "whom" the word is for. If the word is for an individual and you have been released as a prophet in that local assembly by the leadership of that house, then it would be appropriate to go and speak to that individual. In cases where the Lord gives you a word for an individual and you are not released by the leadership of that house, you should and must ***always give respect to that house and its leadership prior to speaking to an individual*** or the body.

<u>Warning</u>: *Protect your anointing by avoiding giving anyone a private prophecy. It was a private prophecy (word) that deceived Eve, but Adam became infected by the private word given because he did not take authority over the serpent.*

It was private prophecy (word) that caused a third of all Moses leadership to fall away. That word was given by Korah.

A private prophecy is an unchecked prophecy and the hearer is at the mercy of the accuracy of that prophetic person. The number one question you have to ask yourself is, are you without error, or one hundred percent on the mark all the time? The answer is undoubtedly No!

Identifying the Recipient of the Word

It is very important to be able to identify the individuals for whom God may give you a word. This takes great discipline because you may receive a word, and it may not be time to give that word to that individual.

<u>Example</u>: *There are times when God may give me a word for someone at the beginning of a service, yet he does not allow me to release that word until the end of the service.*

It takes discipline to hold a prophetic word through the entire service before releasing it. How does one identify the individual that God actually desires to minister to? At the point of you getting up in the morning, expect that there will be a vision, or a word to you, as to who will be in the service that night. Never allow yourself to attempt to become familiar with a place before you have arrived in the place where you are the guest. You should already have lain before the Lord regarding that place, so that when you arrive it is as though you have already been there. At that particular point in time, the faces, images, and surroundings will or should already be familiar to your spirit. This is because you have already lain before the Lord. Once you step into the building, people will stand out to you, regardless of the size of the facility. The most important thing to remember is that your main purpose for going there is to bring forth a word for the house. Along with bringing forth that word, there will be the added benefit of bringing forth a word to an individual.

Remember: *Prophets are ministers to the body of Christ and not just individuals. Therefore, your purpose is to the whole body and not simply to an individual. Whenever prophets try to minister on an individual level only, they limit themselves in many areas and cease from reaching their original purpose.*

It is important that prophetic people understand that they are not above the rules of local assemblies, even if it is the location where they are members. Prophetic people HAVE NO AUTHORITY OR RELEASE TO override the authority of the house.

Overriding authority is one of the ways to stop the flow of the prophetic in your life.

Understand: *Sometimes a word may be for the prophet only and not for others at that time.*

Learning How to Flow Prophetically

Learning Prophetic Order

It is important to understand prophetic order in the local church in order to govern the body accordingly.

The word says that everything should be done decently and in order. The closer to order in the local church, the stronger that prophetic anointing will grow. Therefore, one must understand the methods of prophetic revelation.

Methods of Prophetic Revelation

The Word of God says that He is the same yesterday, today, and forever. Throughout church history we find that God never ceased to relate to his people. The Lord is restoring the power of the Holy Spirit within the church in these last days. As the Lord is pouring forth his spirit, he is bringing a great challenge to the body, to not only pray and sing in the Spirit, but to walk and live in the Spirit. Within this tremendous outpouring, the gifts of the Holy Spirit are becoming more profound within individuals. These experiences are identified as dreams, visions, and written and spoken prophecy.

As we enter this new millennium, the move of the Holy Spirit is bringing prophetic ministries in various forms to be increasingly common in our time. It has become expedient that we, the church, accomplish our purpose in these times.

The ascension gifts are not only scriptural; they were operative throughout Old Testament history, in Jesus' life, and in the life of the early church.

Prophecy, in both the Old and New Testaments, was words inspired by the Spirit of God, and spoken through the utterance of a man or woman for the edification, exhortation, and comfort of the body of

Christ. There are two basic uses for the prophetic. The first is given for revealing the present and future strategic will of God in certain matters. The other is given for the illumination of doctrine that is taught in scripture, but is not clearly seen or clearly understood by the church. These prophetic experiences may be identified in several ways:

1. Prophetic Impressions

There are many levels of prophetic revelation. The beginning levels include prophetic impressions, which are genuine revelations. They can be extraordinarily specific and accurate when interpreted by those who are experienced and sensitive to them. We must be careful, however, at this level, because our own feelings, prejudices, and doctrines can affect our revelations.

Visions can come at the "impression" level, as well. They are gentle and must be seen with the eyes of the heart. They, too, can be very specific and accurate, especially when interpreted by those who are experienced and sensitive to them.

2. Conscious Sense of the Presence of the Lord

There is a level of prophetic revelation that comes as a conscious sense of the presence of the Lord or the anointing of the Holy Spirit. This is when the Holy Spirit gives special illumination to our minds, and will often come when we are writing or speaking. This conscious sense of the presence of the Lord will give greater confidence to the importance or accuracy of what is being spoken. Even at this level the prophet must still be careful about being influenced by his or her own prejudices, doctrines, emotions, and so forth.

3. Open Visions

Open visions occur on a higher level than "impressions." They give more clarity than when we feel the conscious sense of the presence of the Lord, or the anointing. Open visions are external and are viewed with the clarity of a movie screen. We are not able to control them, and there is less change of mixture in revelation that comes through an open vision.

4. Trances

Trances are high levels of prophetic experiences and were common to the biblical prophets. Trances are dreaming when you are awake. Instead of just seeing in the manner of "open visions," a trance is as though you are actually there in the experience. Trances are experiences on different levels. They can be mild. This type of mild stupor allows you to be conscious of your physical surroundings and interact within them.

The next level is where you experience actually being present in the vision. Biblical examples are recorded in the life of Ezekiel and the Apostle John visions recorded in the book of Revelation.

<u>Example</u>: *This is what Peter experienced when the angel led him out of prison. No one ever touched the gates; they opened on their own accord.*

NOTE

SEASON #5
SEASON OF RELEASE

re|lease

vt. -[leased, -[leas[ing *relesen* < OFr *relaisser* < L *relaxare:* see RELAX6

1. to set free, as from confinement, duty, work, etc.

2. to let go or let loose, to *release* an arrow

to grant freedom from a tax, penalty, obligation, etc.

3. 4 to set free from pain, cares, etc.; relieve

4. to permit to be issued, shown, published, broadcast, etc.; put into circulation

5. *Law* to give up or surrender to someone else (a claim, right, etc.)

n.

1. a setting free or being set free; deliverance; liberation

2. a freeing or being freed from a tax, obligation, etc.

3. *a)* a relief from pain, cares, etc. *b)* relief from emotional tension through a spontaneous, uninhibited expression of an emotion

4. a document authorizing release, as from an obligation, from prison, etc.

5. the act of letting loose something caught, held in position, etc.

6. a device to release a catch, etc., as for starting or stopping a machine

7. *a)* the act of releasing a book, film, news story, etc. to the public *b)* the book, film, news story, etc. released

8. *Music a)* the act or method of ending a tone >*b)* the third group of eight measures in a common form of 32-bar chorus, as in a popular tune, which supplies a bridge between repetitions of the melody

9. 9 *Law a)* a giving up or surrender to someone else, as of a claim or right *b)* the document by which this is done; quitclaim

—*SYN* FREE

—taken from *Webster's New World Dictionary*

This is the ultimate season—the grand finale, if you will. This is what most simply cannot wait for. The time to be released is a very sensitive time. If you are released too soon, you can shipwreck. The hand of God is always involved in releasing a person to his or her call. Remember that David could not be released until Samuel spoke and earth agreed. Elisha could not be released until God spoke and Elijah agreed. Joshua could not be released until God spoke and Moses agreed. The definition clearly reveals the idea of being released. However, if we are going to understand the principle of it, we have to see it in the Word.

You can see it in looking at Moses, Elijah, and David's situations.

CHAPTER 6

The Ministry of the Holy Spirit

W e often talk about the Father and about the Son;

but we seldom talk about the Holy Spirit and the Ministry of the Holy Spirit. We don't talk about what his ministry is in the earth and, for that reason, a lot of times many people refer to the Holy Spirit as an "it."

They don't recognize the Holy Spirit as the third person of the Trinity. I would imagine that a lot of people don't necessarily believe in the Trinity, and it is not my goal to discuss the Trinity in this book. It is, however, my goal to give an understanding of whom the Holy Spirit is and what his assignment is in the earth as it relates to the prophet.

The Ministry of the Holy Spirit and Creation

In recognizing the Holy Spirit's assignment as it relates to the prophet, the prophet must first understand that the work of the Holy Spirit did not begin in the Book of Acts. The Holy Spirit has always been here, just as Jesus has always been here and just as the Father has always been here. And although the work of the Holy Spirit really began in eternity past, we will begin our discussion with his involvement in creation. Let's go to Genesis 1.

"In the beginning God created the heaven and the earth. And the earth was without form, and void; and darkness was upon the face of the deep. And the Spirit of God moved upon the face of the waters." Genesis 1:1-2

When reading this portion of scripture, we can begin to understand a facet of the Holy Spirit's assignment. The scripture says that the earth was without form, and it was void. This means that the earth was empty and had no form. Being that the earth had no form; the Holy Spirit's assignment was to bring order to it. How was he to do this? Let's look at verse 2, *"...**And the Spirit of God** [the Holy Spirit] moved upon the face of the waters."* The Holy Spirit was to literally survey the earth at this particular point. Although God was the creator, the Holy Spirit had to first survey what God was about to speak to. So the Holy Spirit surveyed the land, and once he finished, he said to God, "It's now ready." God then spoke into the land, and it became what God declared.

When the Holy Spirit was moving upon the face of the waters, some of us would have tried to erect a building in the water without even hearing from the Holy Spirit. We would have been erecting a building in wetland. Even now, some of us are still trying to build on wet, undeveloped, and underdeveloped land. We're trying to build upon something that has not been surveyed and is not ready to be built upon. Just as God did not and will not speak something into existence until the Holy Spirit has surveyed it, the prophet should never speak anything into someone's life until the Holy Spirit has had an opportunity to survey what is to be spoken to. Once he has surveyed it, the Holy Spirit will then inform God, and God will tell the prophet he can now speak something into existence. Always remember, before God ever creates anything, speaks anything into existence, or moves in the earth, the Holy Spirit must survey it (or scope it out) first. God never does anything until the Holy Spirit has performed his assignment.

Let's look at it this way: If we are going to erect a building, we must first purchase a piece of property. But after we have purchased the property, we still can't just go out and erect the building. The land has to first be surveyed to make sure that the ground can handle the structure of the building that we want to build upon the land. Once the plan has been cleared and given the approval, we can then build upon the land.

Now, I want to ask you a question. What are you building upon? Are you trying to build on something that has not even been surveyed? Are you trying to set some things in place that the Holy Spirit has just shown you but God has not spoken to? Remember, the prophet must always wait on the Holy Spirit.

The Ministry of the Holy Spirit and the Dispensations of Time

Another assignment of the Holy Spirit is to search all things:

> *"But as it is written, <u>Eye hath not seen, nor ear heard, neither have entered into the heart of man, the things which God hath prepared for them that love him</u>. But God hath revealed them unto us by his Spirit: for the Spirit searcheth all things, yea, the deep things of God."*   *1 Corinthians 2:9-10*

The Holy Spirit searches all things. Since dispensations are included in this, it is fair to say that the Holy Spirit searches dispensations. A "dispensation" can be defined as a period or portion of time. As we begin to look further into the ministry of the Holy Spirit, we will understand how God has the ability to declare the end of a thing from the beginning.

Because God understands dispensations, he already knows everything that is going to take place, in which dispensation it's going to come into being and how it's going to come into being. Why? Because the Holy Spirit as the Surveyor, has already searched all those things ahead of time. He has surveyed every period of time so that God will know what he can accomplish in the dispensation in which he is about to create.

In surveying dispensations, the Holy Spirit looked all the way down to the other end of the spectrum and saw what things were to take place. He then communicated the picture of what was surveyed to God. If the Holy Spirit already knows everything that is to happen and at what time it is to happen, then the prophet should always listen to him and be led of him. Prophets should never guess or assume anything.

Dispensations of Time

There are six major dispensations or periods of time. The first dispensation is the Dispensation of Innocence; the second dispensation is called the Dispensation of Conscience; the third is the Dispensation of Civil Government; the fourth dispensation is called the Dispensation of Promise; the fifth dispensation is called the Dispensation of the Law of Israel; and the sixth dispensation is the Dispensation of Grace. We will discuss the first, fifth and sixth dispensations as these periods of time relate to the ministry of the Holy Spirit.

The First Dispensation
The Dispensation of Innocence

This period of time covers Adam and Eve in the Garden of Eden and their relationship with God. During this dispensation, there was no sin in the earth, and authority was given to both Adam and Eve. Being that the Holy Spirit surveyed every dispensation, God knew ahead of time that Adam and Eve were going to miss the mark, when they would miss it, and how they would miss it. However, God didn't become concerned when they missed the mark, nor was God just sitting around, biting his fingernails and wondering whether or not Jesus would finish his assignment. God already knew what great trials Jesus would suffer, but he also knew that Jesus would definitely finish his assignment on this earth. Remember, the Holy Spirit had surveyed this dispensation well in advance.

In addition to surveying dispensations, the Holy Spirit also makes intercession. *"And he that searcheth the heart knoweth what is the mind of the Spirit, because he maketh intercession for the saints according to the will of God"* **(Rom. 8:27).** When Adam and Eve missed the mark, they didn't catch God by surprise because in his mind, the end was already set. God already had a plan set in motion that would rectify Adam and Eve's actions. Isn't it wonderful to know that God was not operating from the mistake that Adam and Eve made, but he was operating from what he knew the end was going to be?

The Fifth Dispensation
The Dispensation of the Law of Israel

The fifth dispensation is the Dispensation of the Law of Israel. This is the dispensation in which Jesus Christ, our Savior, appeared on the scene. His assignment was to save and to redeem that which was lost. Jesus was to set in place what Adam and Eve missed. The ministry of the Holy Spirit was to make sure that all things were known ahead of time, in order to bring fulfillment to God's plan. Because the Holy Spirit surveyed the land, he was able to identify all the weak spots to make sure that God was able to say something that was going to establish or create stability where there was weakness.

The Sixth Dispensation
The Dispensation of Grace

The Dispensation of Grace, which is the sixth dispensation, is where we are in this day, and it is where we (the body of Christ) actually met the Holy Spirit. Please keep in mind that the Holy Spirit was at work in all of the other dispensations, but it is in this Dispensation of Grace that we actually met him. In the Dispensation of Grace, we must free the Holy Spirit so that he can minister to us when he wants to and how he wants to without our questioning him. Let's look at Revelation 1:1 to see an example of the ministry of the Holy Spirit:

> *"The Revelation of Jesus Christ, which God gave unto him, to shew unto his servants things which must shortly come to pass; and he sent and signified it by his angel unto his servant John: Who bare record of the word of God, and of the testimony of Jesus Christ, and of all things that he saw. Blessed is he that readeth, and they that hear the words of this prophecy, and keep those things which are written therein: for the time is at hand."*   Revelation 1:1-3

In addition to the many portions of his service, it is also the Holy Spirit's ministry to keep us on time. Have you ever felt urgency in your spirit and you knew that there was something you had to do? It was the Holy Spirit giving you understanding that at that particular time, you couldn't afford to make another mistake. He was letting you know that the clock was almost down to the last second. Even now, the Holy Spirit is urging us that time is almost up. In this Dispensation of Grace, the Holy Spirit is bringing us to a place of realizing that the Book of Revelation is not something we need to be afraid of. The Book of Revelation (or the Book of Revealed Knowledge) is something we need to understand. It is the Book of that which has been concealed. But now God says, "Look, I want to reveal this to the church."

Let's go to the first chapter of Revelation.

> *"I John, who also am your brother, and companion in tribulation, and in the kingdom and patience of Jesus Christ, was in the isle that is called Patmos, for the word of God, and for the testimony of Jesus Christ. I was in the spirit on the Lord's day, and heard behind me a great voice, as of a trumpet, Saying, I am Alpha and Omega, the first and the last: and, What thou seest, write in a book, and send it unto the seven churches which are in Asia; unto Ephesus, and unto Smyrna, and unto Pergamos, and unto Thyatira, and unto Sardis, and unto Philadelphia, and unto Laodicea. And I turned to see the voice that spake with me. And being turned, I saw seven golden candlesticks;"*
> *Revelation 1:9-12*

The seven golden candlesticks represent the seven churches. Now watch this…

"And in the midst of the seven golden candlesticks one like unto the Son of man, clothed with a garment down to the foot, and girt about the paps with a golden girdle." **(Rev. 1:13).** John saw the Son of man in the midst of the churches. But notice that he said that he (John), "was in the Spirit (Holy Spirit) on the Lord's day," and he turned to see the voice that was speaking. Remember, the Holy Spirit will always go before God speaks. The Holy Spirit had already moved upon the thing that God spoke to. In order for John to hear (in the Holy Spirit) what God was saying or creating, he had to turn around and look back at that which the Holy Spirit had already moved upon.

> *"And I turned to see the voice that spake with me. And being turned, I saw seven golden candlesticks;"*
> *Revelation 1:12*

Although the Holy Spirit had begun searching something else, God was actually talking about what was taking place in the seven churches. Understand that the Holy Spirit had already taken John up to the next place to survey it. We must remember that John's assignment was to say what he saw: "those things which were those things which are, and those things which shall be hereafter." While John was in the Spirit, God began to show him "what shall be." Because of this, John stopped looking at what the Holy Spirit was surveying ahead and turned back to look at the church and to hear what God was saying to her.

Many times prophets can become so engrossed in the things that God shows them will take place in the future that they don't fix the things that are in the past. God doesn't have a problem showing prophets the future. However, he is still going to speak to them regarding those things that are in the past and the present that are in need of repair.

This is another reason that prophets must always yield to the Holy Spirit, and that is because he is always going to have us in a place where we don't really understand. As long as the prophets are in the Holy Spirit, they will always enter into unfamiliar places. Why? Because the Holy Spirit goes into action before God speaks into a thing.

Please keep in mind that although the Holy Spirit has already gone and surveyed something, he is not trying to set up anything. The Holy Spirit is only surveying. This is an area where many prophets make a huge mistake. Because the Holy Spirit has taken them somewhere and shown them some things, prophets often attempt to set things in place before God has spoken. Prophets must always turn around and see what God says.

When God speaks concerning the past, he is encouraging or helping the prophet to close doors that should no longer be opened. When God speaks regarding the present, he moves the prophet to fix some things. The prophet can never build upon the future if he has never repaired the things in the present. And, the prophet can't even begin to fix the things in the present if he doesn't close the door to things in the past.

Let's move on to Revelation 2:

"Unto the angel of the church of Ephesus write; These things saith he that holdeth the seven stars in his right hand, who walketh in the midst of the seven golden candlesticks; I know thy works, and thy labour, and thy patience, and how thou canst not bear them which are evil: and thou hast tried them which say they are apostles, and are not, and hast found them liars: And hast borne, and hast patience, and for my name's sake hast laboured, and hast not fainted. Nevertheless I have somewhat against thee, because thou hast left their first love. Remember therefore from whence thou art fallen, and repent, and do the first works; or else I will come unto thee quickly, and will remove thy candlestick out of his place, except thou repent."
Revelation 2:1-5

The seven stars are the seven angels of the church, and the seven candlesticks represent the seven churches. The word "angel" comes from the word "angelos," which is where we get the word "ministers." The angels of the church are the pastors or bishops of those churches. They are not angels who are going to fly, but they are ministering angels that God has set in the church.

Every one of these churches discussed in the Book of Revelation can be found in our day because the Book of Revelation takes place in the Dispensation of Grace.

In other words, the seven churches are still in the Dispensation of Grace. Being that they are in this particular dispensation, we must understand that God is saying, "Look, even though I have already shown you the land that is up ahead, you must still fix the things that are in the present." The assignment now is to repent and to return to your first love, Jesus Christ. Repent and do the first works all over again.

What are the first works? The first works are repentance. At this point God starts to bring the church to a place of repentance. We can even go back to Adam and see a correlation. Adam had to do a work of repentance because he moved from his place of grace. God had given him certain privileges and authority, but he left his first love—God—to follow in the direction of another—Satan. Adam had to repent and turn back to God. In the same manner, God says to the church at Ephesus (and to us), "I want you to fix the fact that you have left your first love." How is that done? You fix leaving your first love by repentance. You repent and do your first works over.

> "Remember therefore from whence thou art fallen, and repent, and do the first works; or else I will come unto thee quickly, and will remove thy candlestick out of his place, except thou repent. But this thou hast, that thou hatest the deeds of the Nicolaitans, which I also hate."　　　　　　　　　　　　　　　　　Revelation 2:5-6

God is going to say this to nearly every church, "He that hath an ear, let him hear what the Spirit saith unto the churches." Remember, the job of the Holy Spirit is to **survey**. Therefore, he had already surveyed this particular church. He then tells this church exactly where their failures were so that they can deal with them.

We can't effectively operate in the ministry of the Holy Spirit if we won't deal with the areas in which we have failed. Why? We can become vulnerable in any area of failure by spending too much time focusing on the fact that we failed. To tell the truth, if we focus too much in three specific areas, we can hinder the ministry of the Holy Spirit.

Those three areas are:

* Failures
* Weaknesses
* Strengths

We can focus so much on our weaknesses that those weaknesses begin to get the best of us. And, as foolish as it may sound, we can even become vulnerable to our strengths. If we spend too much time focusing on our strengths, we can operate in a spirit of pride. The Bible says, *"Wherefore let him that thinketh he standeth take heed lest he fall"* (**1 Cor. 10:12**).

Quenching the Ministry of the Holy Spirit

A prophet must always remember that the ministry of the Holy Spirit has always been and is always in motion. His ministry will never be at a standstill. Because the Holy Spirit is always moving, the prophet must always be in tune with him. The prophet should never quench the Holy Spirit. And although we know that the body of Christ should be yielded to the Holy Spirit, somewhere along the line we have moved above and beyond the Holy Spirit.

Our "religion" has basically shut down the ministry of the Holy Spirit in the earth and has placed him on the shelf. We're trying to do the work of the Holy Spirit ourselves, thereby operating according to our flesh. Listen; when we declare that we don't need apostles and prophets and that we don't need any of the gifts of the Spirit, we have quenched the ministry of the Holy Spirit. When we profess that we do not need "tongues," unknowingly we are dismissing the ministry of the Holy Spirit. When we believe that we no longer need to pray in the Spirit, we are saying that we do not need the Holy Spirit to pray or intercede through us.

If you don't believe in speaking in an unknown tongue, you have dismissed the ministry of the Holy Spirit.

"And suddenly there came a sound from heaven as of a rushing mighty wind, and it filled all the house where they were sitting. And there appeared unto them cloven tongues like as of fire, and it sat upon each of them. And they were all filled with the Holy Ghost, and began to speak with other tongues, as the Spirit gave them utterance."   *Acts 2:2-4*

They were all filled with the Holy Ghost and began to speak in other tongues as the Spirit (the Holy Spirit) gave them utterance. That's what we have to understand. It's the Holy Spirit who comes in to give the utterance, but you have to speak. The Holy Spirit is not going to hit you upside your head and make you speak.

On the inside of you, where the Holy Spirit does his ministry, you'll hear tongues that the Holy Spirit is literally speaking at that particular moment, and you will just say what he says. This is the ministry of the Holy Spirit, and God wants each and every one of us to operate in this area. He wants the Holy Spirit to have the opportunity to minister through us.

"For he that speaketh in an unknown tongue speaketh not unto men, but unto God: for no man understandeth him; howbeit, in the spirit he speaketh mysteries."   *1 Corinthians 14:2*

Here's the exciting part about this: Unknown tongues is a natural language that you have never learned. I believe that when we're speaking in unknown tongues, ministry is able to come through the body of Christ. I also believe that when we are speaking in an unknown tongue, we are ministering to someone who speaks that particular language and understands everything that God is saying.

If people are in your midst who can't speak your language, the Holy Spirit wants to minister to them. He doesn't want them to come in and just hear us speak in English and have their understanding be unfruitful. They would have no idea what we were saying. If we don't yield to the ministry of the Holy Spirit, they will come into our midst and will leave the same way they came in. But, if we yield to the Holy Spirit, we will speak something in their language so that they will understand. If not, the Holy Spirit will give them a supernatural ability to interpret what we are saying in English, having never learned our language. God will then get the credit because we yielded ourselves to the Holy Spirit.

Imagine what would take place during praise and worship if everyone, including the musicians, would come to every service and say, "Today, I release myself to the Holy Spirit." My God, praise and worship would be awesome! Do you realize that releasing ourselves to the Holy Spirit would tap us into things that we couldn't possibly accomplish on our own?

Another facet of the Holy Spirit's ministry is to interpret what was spoken in tongues.

If we were to receive interpretation of the tongues that we had spoken, we would be amazed at the many mysteries that would be unfolded.

We've been asking God questions and have declared, "But God hasn't given me an answer yet." Well, yes he did. We just didn't know what he said when he answered us. We thought that it thundered when it was actually God who had spoken. Why? We dismissed the ministry of the Holy Spirit.

Do you pray in the Spirit? If not, you have dismissed yet another area of the ministry of the Holy Spirit.

When we pray in the Holy Spirit, there are some things that God—through and by the Holy Spirit—uses us to pray for although our mind is unfruitful to what we are praying.

"Likewise the Spirit also helpeth our infirmities: for we know not what we should pray for as we ought: but the Spirit itself maketh intercession for us with groanings which cannot be uttered. And he that searcheth the hearts knoweth what is the mind of the Spirit, because he maketh intercession for the saints according to the will of God." Romans 8:26-27

The Holy Ghost can't minister from the outside. He's got to minister from inside of us in order to minister effectively. In the same manner, the prophet will not be able to effectively minister if he's on the outside of someone's problem.

Let's say, for instance, I know that Suzie has a serious problem that she's dealing with. Now, because I don't like her problem and don't want to be involved with it, I separate myself from Suzie. By doing this, I have just locked myself out of allowing the Holy Spirit to work through me to help Suzie. In order for the Holy Spirit to minister to Suzie, I've got to get with her and beckon God on her behalf.

Again, the Holy Spirit doesn't work from the outside, he works from the inside. Once a prophet excludes himself from someone who has a problem, he has locked himself and the Holy Spirit out from helping that person.

"For I reckon that the sufferings of this present time are not worthy to be compared with the glory which shall be revealed in us. For the earnest expectation of the creature waiteth for the manifestation of the sons of God. For the creature was made subject to vanity, not willingly, but by reason of him who hath subjected the same, in hope, Because the creature itself also shall be delivered from the bondage of corruption into the glorious liberty of the children of God." Romans 8:18-21

God never goes forth on a "might." He never goes on a "you *should* be delivered." God pronounces, *"...the creature itself also **shall be delivered** from the bondage of corruption into the glorious liberty of the children of God."*

Let's read a little further into the ministry of the Holy Spirit.

"For we know that the whole creation groaneth and travaileth in pain together until now. And not only they, but ourselves also, which have the firstfruits of the Spirit, even we ourselves groan within ourselves, waiting for the adoption, to wit, the redemption of our body. For we are saved by hope: but hope that is seen is not hope: for what a man seeth, why doth he yet hope for? But if we hope for that we see not, then do we with patience wait for it. Likewise the Spirit also helpeth our infirmities: for we know not what we should pray for as we ought: but the Spirit itself maketh intercession for us with groanings which cannot be uttered. And he that searcheth the hearts knoweth what is the mind of the Spirit, because he maketh intercession for the saints according to the will of God. And we know that all things work together for good to them that love God, to them who are the called according to his purpose. For whom he did foreknow, he also did predestinate to be conformed to the image of his Son, that he might be the firstborn among many brethren. Moreover whom he did predestinate, them he also called: and whom he called, them he also justified: and whom he justified, them he also glorified."

Romans 8:22-30

God would love for us to understand what it was that we prayed for in the Spirit realm. However, he cannot allow us to understand what we prayed because we would then begin to walk in doubt and unbelief. Therefore, God only wants us to be an instrument through which the Holy Spirit prays because there are particular things that he can't get done in heaven. It has to come from the ministry of the Holy Spirit in the earth. When you pray in the Spirit, you have no idea what is actually taking place in the spirit realm. One

thing is certain: the Enemy's intentions are being overthrown! Hallelujah!

As prophets of God, it is imperative that we be led by the Holy Spirit and not by our flesh. We've got to step aside and yield to the ministry of the Holy Spirit. If only we would just yield to him, he would literally take over and the ministry of the prophet would be very effective in the earth.

Being With One Accord

God waits for us to come into oneness so that the Holy Spirit can move *suddenly*!

"And when the day of Pentecost was fully come, they were all with one accord in one place. And suddenly there came a sound from heaven as of a rushing mighty wind, and it filled all the house where they were sitting." Acts 2:1-2

They were all with one accord and in one place. If we're ever going to see the full bloom of the ministry of the Holy Spirit, we have to be with one accord and in one place. *"And **suddenly** there came a sound from heaven..."* This is the exact way that we're to expect the Holy Ghost to move. And guess what, if we're all expecting on that level, then he will show up on that level.

The Holy Spirit doesn't want to creep in. Contrary to popular belief, the Holy Spirit doesn't like landing that way. If we look at the ministry of the Holy Spirit in the Gospels, he never sneaks in. When we're yielding to the ministry of the Holy Spirit, if we need a healing, he doesn't like to creep healing in—that's not his best style. The Holy Spirit likes to bring in that healing **suddenly**! **"All I know**

is that once I was blind and now I see." Did you get that?
"That's all I know." He didn't say, "Once I was blind and
then gradually my sight came back." **"I was here and then
I was there."** The Holy Spirit never comes in quietly. He
likes to come in with a bang—suddenly!

We're in that day where the Holy Spirit wants to minister to
us. I believe with all of my heart that the Holy Spirit is tired
of seeing men and women operate in their flesh. He's tired
of seeing a lot of "gradual" things that hinder him from
moving the way he wants. I believe that when the Holy
Ghost comes in, he wants to come in **suddenly!** He wants
to come in with a big bang!

Now hear this prophecy: "If we dare to bring ourselves into
absolute oneness, releasing the ministry of the Holy Spirit,
I guarantee you that there will be many days when pastors
all over the world will not even be able to preach on
Sunday mornings. There will be such a powerful move of
the Holy Spirit that, with our own ears, we will hear angels
singing. We will hear instruments we've never heard in the
earth. The most awesome choir that you would ever want to
hear is in heaven."

The Building Process

The ministry of the Holy Spirit is not something that just
automatically happens in the prophet's life. The prophet
must position himself or herself to receive the ministry of
the Holy Spirit. God has predestined every prophet, as well
as the body of Christ, to yield to the ministry of the Holy
Spirit. If Jesus had not yielded to the ministry of the Holy
Spirit, he could never have done what he did in the earth.
However, because Jesus yielded to Holy Spirit, he had the

ability to do what many people thought could not be done. He was able to do what some people said hadn't been done in the earth up to that point. In the Gospels, we read where it was said, "We have never heard anyone speak in this fashion. Never have we seen anyone that opened blind eyes. Never have we seen deaf ears unstopped. Never have we seen a man who is able to speak to the seas and the elements and have things begin to happen. Never have we seen any of these things."

Is there ever a time when the ministry of the Holy Spirit will not be able to work for the prophet?

Whenever the prophet comes to the place where he is trying to minister outside of what is recognized as *his* Jerusalem, he has moved out of order, and the ministry of the Holy Spirit will not be able to work.

The Holy Spirit desires to start exactly where we live. We must start first with our Jerusalem, second with our Judaea, third with our Samaria, and, last of all, with our uttermost parts of the earth. A lot of us try to love everybody first and we neglect to even try to love our own home. Then we want to yield ourselves to the ministry of the Holy Spirit. See, if the Holy Spirit is working in your own home, he will work anywhere. I say this because your home is the hardest place to win because the ministry of the Holy Spirit wants to win you first. Let the ministry of the Holy Spirit work on you.

Let's go back to Acts 2. In this particular chapter, the ministry of the Holy Spirit comes into full bloom. Why? The answer is that the ministry of the Holy Spirit is not just trying to bless you and your family. The Holy Spirit thinks larger than that. The Holy Spirit thinks outside of the box, not in the box.

In addition, a prophet must never become discouraged due to his current state because God never becomes discouraged by what he sees. Why? The Holy Spirit has already surveyed us, and God is looking at the end product. Based on what the Holy Spirit saw, God will speak. Here's the question: Are you really ready to hear what God is going to say based upon what the Holy Spirit has shown him concerning you? If the Holy Spirit sees you as you are, can God really build on you? Understand, it is the Holy Spirit who surveys us; but it is God's desire to build upon us. The Holy Spirit comes in to survey the ground and to determine whether or not we can be built upon. If we can't, then there is a process we must go through.

There are some very specific steps in this process. First, we're going to have to pace ourselves. Then, as we are pacing ourselves, God builds us up in every area where we are lacking. The areas where we are lacking will determine how long the process will be. What are you going through right now, and how long have you been going through it? The length of time that you've been going through can be an indication of the size of the ministry that God wants to use you in.

We should never judge people because they have been going through for a long time. You have no clue what God is doing in them. Likewise, we should never mumble and complain because we have been going through for a long time. God is doing something, and once we understand this, once we really identify with what God is doing in this particular hour, we will more readily yield to the Holy Spirit because he will allow us to be processed in an adequate amount of time. Once the process is complete, we will then move into what God has spoken regarding our lives.

Waiting on the Holy Spirit

When the prophet yields to the Holy Spirit, he will realize that he is actually *waiting* on the Holy Spirit, which is another component of the building process.

How do we know that you have really yielded to the ministry of the Holy Spirit if the thing has always been working? All you had to do was to keep on working the thing that was already working. How do we know that you had the power of God working on the inside of you? How do we know that you've fasted and that you've prayed and that you've stayed in the face of God? How do we know that? The fact is we don't. But when you take something that is broken and you're in the face of the Holy Spirit, when the Holy Spirit says, "Just wait." Then all of a sudden he speaks to you and says, "Here is what I want you to do." and the thing comes back working. Now we know that you are in touch with God! But, we all must first wait.

"And, being assembled together with them, commanded them that they should not depart from Jerusalem, but wait for the promise of the Father, which, saith he, ye have heard of me." Acts 1:4

Now lock this in right here. One of the components in the building process is *waiting*. Understand this: the Holy Spirit is getting ready to survey the thing, so when God begins to speak, there will be instant results. As the prophet begins to wait, he's actually waiting on the promise of the Father. This is one of the most difficult things for a prophet to do. However, during this period of waiting, we have seen people move from the status of being disabled to being able. This is during the period where we have seen people who had AIDS be healed. Listen, the Holy Spirit had already surveyed this thing, and he moved us into a place of waiting.

Sadly, during this period, we begin to act out of the will of God and call prayer lines. Now, I'm not saying there's anything wrong with calling a prayer line, I just don't call them when people think that I should call one. If I call a prayer line and God has not told me to call it, then I need to heal everyone in that line. But if God says, "Call a prayer line," then the only thing that I need to do is show up. If God tells me to lay hands on the people in the prayer line, then I will lay hands on them and expect the Holy Spirit to heal them. Because God said to lay hands on them, they will get healed right in the line. If God tells a prophet to let people touch the hem of his coat to receive their healing, then everyone who touches the hem of the prophet's coat will be healed. Why? Because this is not about us, but it is all about what the Holy Spirit is doing, and he is the one who shines.

I believe that we have stepped into a period of time where God is saying, "Look, stop showing what you want to show and yield to the Holy Spirit. Let him do his assignment in the earth, and Jesus will confirm it with signs." Jesus is not going to confirm you.

Leaving Your Comfort Zone

When yielding to the Holy Spirit, the prophet will have to abandon his or her comfort zone.

"Nevertheless I tell you the truth; It is expedient for you that I go away: for if I go not away, the Comforter will not come unto you;..."
John 16:7

In other words, the one who is designed to help you cannot even come to you if your comfort zone does not go away. Jesus was the disciples' comfort zone. Like the disciples, the prophet must abandon his comfort zone. The Holy Spirit has already surveyed all that is ahead of you. God has your back regardless of where you are. The prophet must abandon everything that he has trusted in and every support system that he has. He must totally rely upon God as his support system.

Jesus said to the disciples, "It is expedient for you that I go away." Or, in simpler terms, "It is vitally important for you that I leave." Jesus had been walking with the disciples a long time, and he was everything to them. They had slept together, eaten together, and done everything together. Jesus taught the disciples everything that they knew, and now he told them that he had to leave them. Can you imagine how they felt? He was forcing the disciples out of their comfort zone.

Often, God has to allow things to happen in prophets' lives to back them into a corner and force them out of their comfort zone. Even now, some of you may be wondering why someone walked out on you. It was more profitable to you for them to leave. They, not God, were meeting your every need. They were the ones who showed up every time you raised your hand and sweated just a little bit. God was told, "Sit down right here and I'll be back on Sunday." But God said, "Look, I want to be a part of your life every day that you breathe. I want to be the one who will meet your needs." For this reason, God had to allow that person to walk out on you so that he could show up in your life. He had to become your support system.

Just as the disciples were forced to trust in a power they could not see, prophets must do the same. They must place their trust and confidence in the power of God.

Classified Information

> *"Howbeit we speak wisdom among them that are perfect: yet not the wisdom of this world, nor of the princes of this world, that come to nought; But we speak the wisdom of God in a mystery, even the hidden wisdom, which God ordained before the world unto our glory; Which none of the princes of this world knew: for had they known it, they would not have crucified the Lord of glory. But as it is written, Eye hath not seen, nor ear heard, neither have entered into the heart of man, the things which God hath prepared for them that love him. But God hath revealed them unto us by his Spirit: for the Spirit searcheth all things, yea, the deep things of God."*
> *1 Corinthians 2:6-10*

There is classified information that God wants to reveal to the prophet, as well as the body of Christ, into. The world has never been able to tap into this information, nor will it ever be able to do so. This is the reason that we need to stop fussing and fighting with people of the world and stop trying to get them to understand the Bible. The Bible **is classified information** for a classified group of people.

There is another level of information that is going to come through the prophet. God is going to allow us to speak some things and get it instantaneously. We are about to enter into a realm with God where we are going to be able to get some things just by thinking about them based upon the information received. Up to this point, we have been getting things based upon what we ask for. But, God is saying to the prophet, "Look, I'm getting ready to tap you into another realm of information." I'm telling you right now in Jesus' name, the only thing that prophets are going to have to do is think about the thing and the thing is going to show up! We have got to get ready for this move of God.

Let's recall something that Jesus said to the disciples:

"I have yet many things to say unto you, but ye cannot bear them now." *John 16:12*

Yielding to the Holy Spirit also means that you will **not** come into information before it is time for you to come into it. Jesus told the disciples, "I have some things I want to share with you, but you can't [handle] them right now."

The Holy Spirit surveys the prophets to find out whether they can handle information that God wants to release to them. If the prophets can't handle it at that time, he won't tell or release it to them. However, God will not change his mind about releasing that bit of information to the prophets. Instead, he builds the prophets up to a point where they can handle (or receive) it.

Prophets of God, when God releases information to you, it says that you are authorized to know that information and that God can trust you to keep it confidential. When God releases you to do so, you will be able to use that information and speak to the unclean and command them to be clean. And because you released classified information to the right source at the right time, that unclean person will become clean.

If we go back to what God did in the Book of Genesis, we will have a better understanding of the ministry of the Holy Spirit. We will better understand that the Holy Spirit gives us information to speak forth that can transform things that are without form, are void, are empty, and have darkness upon them.

> *"And God said, Let us make man in our image, after our likeness: and let them have dominion over the fish of the sea, and over the fowl of the air, and over the cattle, and over all the earth, and over every creeping thing that creepeth upon the earth. So God created man in his own image, in the image of God created he him; male and female created he them."* Genesis 1:26-27

> *"And the Lord God formed man of the dust of the ground, and breathed into his nostrils the breath of life; and man became a living soul."* Genesis 2:7

You are going to find that when the Holy Spirit wants to do something and when God wants to manifest his power in the earth, he'll always start off with something that is empty, is without form, and has darkness upon it. We want to start out with something that is already working, but God is saying, "Look, I want you to start out with something that is *broken.*"

We can't give up on someone just because darkness is upon him or her. While it is correct that God doesn't want us to hang around darkness, we must realize that he wants us to speak to the darkness and command light to come forth so that the person will be transformed by the life that came out of our mouths because we breathed on them.

What does it mean to "breathe" upon someone? We have witnessed what seems to be a trend in the body of Christ of people breathing or blowing upon others.

The word "to breathe" comes from the Hebrew word "ruach" and it means, "to blow into." You are not going to look at what's on the outside and blow into it. You are going to look at what is on the inside, and then you are going to reach on the inside and blow into the thing so that it becomes what you said. This breathing is not a physical act.

Are you ready for this? We, as prophets, are going to have to go back to some of those drug-infested men and women, and instead of breathing into them, "You are a drug addict" or, "You are a prostitute,"

...we will take hold of them and say exactly what God said.

As you look inside of that drug-infested man, that drug-infested woman, that prostituting son and daughter, "Ruach" on the inside of them and breathe, "You are a man of God!" Breathe, "You are what God says you are!" Breathe upon them, "You are a preacher of the living God!" And then they will become.

The pattern for performing this task is found in the book of beginnings. In Genesis 1 we find the words, *"In the beginning God created the heaven and the earth."*

Listen, God shows up on the scene and makes dirt into a man. The Holy Spirit does not come on the scene until it is time to inflate him, this dirt man. What is it that God is expecting to inflate through you? The thing surely will be inflated, but what it is inflated with is determined by what you say. It is the ministry of the Holy Spirit.

Oftentimes we arrive at a place where we say things that God doesn't want said. God wants some things said that will inflate people with what he says and with what he saw. We said earlier that the thing would surely be inflated, but will it be inflated with all that God is? Or, will it be inflated with our minute and limited thoughts of what they could be?

"In the beginning God created the heaven and the earth. And the earth was without form..." Those you will encounter have no form. They have no shape. They are empty-headed. What are you going to do with what God said to you? With what God has shown you? It is time now for us to reach on the inside and pour out of us, to blow up or "ruach" out of us, exactly what God showed us that he wanted in the earth.

We need to begin to say what God is saying because as prophets of God, we can have exactly what we say. So, I just choose to say what God said. And you know what? When it comes down to my home, do you know what I say? I say the same thing that God said, *"Great shall be the peace of my children and in righteousness shall they be established."* It doesn't mean that I don't have to correct them. It doesn't mean that I don't have to do whatever it is that I need to do to drive out anything that looks wrong out of there. What it means is, *"Great shall be the peace of my children and in righteousness shall they be established,"* just as God has already said.

NOTE

CHAPTER
7

How to Walk and Operate in Your Office

Prophets are what I call God's special agents, and

unless we learn how to operate, we will never experience all of the fullness of God. I want to share with you some of my personal experiences and things I had to endure as a budding prophet. We also want to talk about some of the "Prophetic hazards" a prophet must avoid.

Know To Whom You Are Called

Find the people that you are called to – Everybody is not called to everybody. We have to know the people that we are called to and stick with them. One example is found in John 5:1-9:

"After this there was a feast of the Jews; and Jesus went up to Jerusalem. 2 Now there is at Jerusalem by the sheep market a pool, which is called in the Hebrew tongue Bethesda, having five porches. 3 In these lay a great multitude of impotent folk, of blind, halt, withered, waiting for the moving of the water. 4 For an angel went down at a certain season into the pool, and troubled the water: whosoever then first after the troubling of the water stepped in was made whole of whatsoever disease he had. 5 And a certain man was there, which had an infirmity thirty and eight years. 6 When Jesus

saw him lie, and knew that he had been now a long time in that case, he saith unto him, Wilt thou be made whole? 7 The impotent man answered him, Sir, I have no man, when the water is troubled, to put me into the pool: but while I am coming, another steppeth down before me. 8 Jesus saith unto him, Rise, take up thy bed, and walk. 9 And immediately the man was made whole, and took up his bed, and walked: and on the same day was the sabbath."　　　*John 5:1-9*

There were many sick people there; this was like a convalescent home. And Jesus as kind and loving as He is, left all of the other sick people there, the way that they were when He came in. Jesus left after he healed this one person. How could Jesus, who had the ability to heal all of these people, walk out without healing the others? Jesus was not called to the others.

Another example is found in Acts 3:1-9 & 3:1:

"Now Peter and John went up together into the temple at the hour of prayer, being the ninth hour. 2 And a certain man lame from his mother's womb was carried, whom they laid daily at the gate of the temple which is called Beautiful, to ask alms of them that entered into the temple; 3 Who seeing Peter and John about to go into the temple asked an alms. 4 And Peter, fastening his eyes upon him with John, said, Look on us. 5 And he gave heed unto them, expecting to receive something of them. 6 Then Peter said, Silver and gold have I none; but such as I have give I thee: In the name of Jesus Christ of Nazareth rise up and walk. 7 And he took him by the right hand, and lifted him up: and immediately his feet and ankle bones received strength. 8 And he leaping up stood, and walked, and entered with them into the temple, walking, and leaping, and praising God. 9 And all the people saw him walking and praising God:" Acts 3:1-9 & 3:1

This lame man was daily at the gate. Jesus passes this person every time He went into the temple. He did what He needed to do, and walked out past that person and did not heal him. This person was not Jesus' assignment. He was Peter and John's assignment. Jesus would not touch Peter and John's assignment. We should not touch people that are not our assignment. We have an anointing to minister to people that are our assignment, but we do not have an anointing for people that are not our assignment. Sometimes we get attacked by demonic forces, because we are handling something that we are not called to dominate. How can you be anointed and get defeated? This can happen if we are operating in an area that is not our assignment. Find the people that you are called to, and work with them. Do not try to work in someone else's area, even if you think that it will make you look good on your spiritual resume.

Know Where You Are Called

The next thing that I encourage people to do is find the place that you are called to. The place where you are now, – are you there because you are familiar with them? Are you there because that is where your family has always been? Did you hear God say this is your place of purpose? You have to be sure that this is your place of purpose. This is a hard decision to make. You need to know exactly where you are called. Let me give you a hint, so you will be able to determine if you are in the right place. It is not my job to tell you where you should be. Do not ask me, because I am not going to answer that question. It would not be fair to you or to your pastor, for me to answer that question. However, I have to give you the information. So that you can start thinking about it, and get an understanding about whether or not you are in the right place, to enhance what God has called you to do. This is something that I would talk about very prayerfully. Because the last thing that I would want you to do, is to uproot yourself, at a moment when God is planting some stuff in you.

If you are saying that the place where I am now is too difficult, that is not a good reason to leave, because prophets have to be raised up in a place like Ramah of Gilead, which is a high and rough place. Prophets are not raised down by the still waters. You were by the still water when you were a lamb, and a sheep. But now that you are a prophetic voice, you are up on the mountain, where there was an earthquake, a strong wind and a fire shooting, and that is where you grow. I need something that is going to push me, when I feel that I can't take it anymore. I need something that is going to challenge me right there. You need to be at a place that will push you, when you think that you can't take any more.

When we begin to think about the places that we are called to, now we understand how our prophetic is going to work, because the place that is feeding me is also cutting me. It is time out for being a jellybean, because at one point or another, you are going to have to be circumcised. You have to be willing to sit still long enough to allow somebody to cut you.

Prophets have to be cut. A prophet that is not cut, normally withers away. Why do we need that? It is because God is going to give us a word that is not a comfortable word. Now when we are lambs or sheep, we normally need confirmation so that we can know that we are doing the right things, based on the level of comfort. That is not necessarily a fact for a prophet. Comfort is not a confirmation to the prophet's office, neither is chaos.

How do we measure this, we measure it by the Spirit of the Living God. We do everything by the word of God. I had to learn this the hard way, so that I would not make decisions based on the level of comfort, or based on the level of conflict. Let us take a look at this in 1 Kings 17:1-5:

> *"And Elijah the Tishbite, who was of the inhabitants of Gilead, said unto Ahab, As the LORD God of Israel liveth, before whom I stand, there shall not be dew nor rain these years, but according to my word. 2 And the word of the LORD came unto him, saying, 3 Get thee hence, and turn thee eastward, and hide thyself by the brook Cherith, that is before Jordan. 4 And it shall be, that thou shalt drink of the brook; and I have commanded the ravens to feed thee there. 5 So he went and did according unto the word of the LORD: for he went and dwelt by the brook Cherith, that is before Jordan. 6 And the ravens brought him bread and flesh in the morning, and bread and flesh in the evening; and he drank of the brook."*   *1 Kings 17:1-5*

Remember, you have to be where God told you to be, in order to get your mail. Now take a look at this; if God told Elijah to be at the brook Cherith, that is where he had to be, not at any other brook, he had to be at that particular one. The ravens that devoured everything had a nature change; not all of the ravens, just those that were assigned to Elijah, only those.

I am absolutely convinced that the reason that some things that you and I are believing God for, have not manifested, is because we were not at the place where we were supposed to be, at the time that we were supposed to be there. Remember, if God specified the brook, then Elijah needed to go there, if he was going to eat. That was his place of purpose and it was called "there." This is a prophetic test! You as a prophet are being tested. In the initial stage this is what happens, God allows a whirlwind to be going on in your head. You have to be in the storm and still able to hear Him. Then the test of direction comes, and you now have to follow the direction that you heard from God. What is literally happening is that you are hearing God, but the test is "I want to hear the way that I am used to hearing, because that is comfortable for me." And God is trying to get you to hear on the next level. So Elijah is really going through a real test here, because he is worn out at this point. Have you ever been worn out? I know that I have. It is at that state that God allows our hearing to be tested. What He is really doing is putting us on the right course, and giving us a level of confidence, that our hearing is on point. I am able to understand this, because this is the direction that He tested and took me.

Every prophet has to go thru this, and not one will escape it. The only ones that escape this are the ones that are not even close, to hearing with one hundred percent accuracy. So when we try to escape this, we miss hearing God. We miss it. Remember, God will change the nature of stuff, if you and I will dare to obey Him. If we decide to obey God, He will change the nature of things. What is tested is your hearing, when you make the decision to obey God, and the Devil will tempt you at that point. Jesus decided to obey God and go to be baptized by John the Baptist, and immediately after that, He was led into the wilderness to be tempted by the Devil. Therefore, your ability and my ability to hear God are connected with our decisions. The Devil has to understand that I decided to hear God on this one, and it's too late for him. You tell the Devil that it is too late. Now God gets involved and He will bring you a word, at any given moment, so that you can obey Him. We have to avail ourselves to God like that, for Him to respond to us that way.

Let's look at ***Rev. 3:20: "Behold, I stand at the door, and knock: if any man hear my voice, and open the door, I will come in to him, and will sup with him, and he with me."*** Jesus says here, if any man will hear. He is talking about anybody. Whenever you see "if" in the Bible, look for the blessing that follows, because it is contingent on obedience of what He said. This turns out to be a principle that every prophet has to walk through. Let's number what happens in the principle of this passage: You have to obey two things, before you get the blessing (1) If any man hears my voice (2) and open the door. Obedience causes you to receive the three part blessing, associated with your obedience of hearing His voice, and opening the door. The three part blessing is (1) He will come in, (2) He will sup with you, and (3) you will sup with Him. This is going to cause God to wake you up at night to pray. Now we talked about this some time ago in ***Heb. 3:15: "While it is said, Today if ye will hear his voice, harden not your hearts, as in the provocation."*** When God wakes you up, you can't harden your heart and not get up. You can harden your heart in your sleep, not literally in your sleep, but when you wake up, you decide, "I don't want to get up." You harden your heart; but you have to give God permission, every single time that He wants to talk to you. God knows that when you make a decision to get up, He has your attention.

What happens to the voice of God at this point? The voice of God starts to grow stronger and stronger, and then you get to the point that you hear God, while other people are talking to you. You hear God in your spirit, and you hear the person that you are talking to with your natural ears. You don't have to shut God down, so that you can hear the person that you are talking to. This will take some discipline, but when you step into the office of the Prophet, you have to be able to do that like clockwork. Here is the rest of this: If you open the door, what you are doing, is allowing God to come in, at any given moment.

My wife has gotten me into watching movies, because there was a time that I did not go to the movies. I did not look at them, nor did I watch television. It was all Jesus for me. Now if movies are your weakness, don't you try this. I did not have that problem. I watch movies because my wife likes movies. One night we were watching a particular movie, and I got stuck on something that God spoke to me during that movie. I was able to watch the movie, but God gave me a revelation of the twelve disciplines of faith, and the corresponding scriptures to prove the twelve disciplines. He said if you don't have it, you will not be able to work anything supernaturally, and get instant results (if you do not master the twelve disciplines of faith). God used this crazy movie, to speak to me. I open the door to Him and He knows that He can speak to me at any given moment.

Why is God so serious about talking to us, and us hearing and obeying what He tells us? It is because there is a preceding and a proceeding word from God. The obedience of your preceding word will bring you to the manifestation of your proceeding word. Remember God said to Abraham in *Gen. 22:2: "And he said, Take now thy son, thine only son Isaac, whom thou lovest, and get thee into the land of Moriah; and offer him there for a burnt offering upon one of the mountains which I will tell thee of.*" This was a preceding word to Abraham. Now Abraham had more than one son, he had another son, Ishmael that was born before Isaac; but God did not recognize him. God called Isaac his only son. God is not recognizing everything that we do. He only recognizes what He tells us to do, not what we may come up with. I feel sorry for preachers who get off course, because they have buddies that are doing this or that. Their buddies may be doing day care and that is bringing in thousands of dollars every week, and that may make sense when you look at the income, but that may not be God's purpose for you. It is a breeze for them, because God told them to do it. You try to do it and you struggle at it, because that is not God's purpose for your life. So when God sees you doing what He did not tell you to do, He says that is an Ishmael. Where is the one thing that I told you to do? What did I call you to do? Where is that?

The prophet has to have a right now word, and it may be a preceding or a proceeding word. After Abraham obeyed the preceding word, we see that in Gen. 22:9-12:

"And they came to the place which God had told him of; and Abraham built an altar there, and laid the wood in order, and bound Isaac his son, and laid him on the altar upon the wood. 10 And Abraham stretched forth his hand, and took the knife to slay his son. 11 And the angel of the LORD called unto him out of heaven, and said,...." Genesis 22:9-12

Now after this act of obedience Abraham get his proceeding word.

> *"Abraham, Abraham: and he said, Here am I. 12 And he said, Lay not thine hand upon the lad, neither do thou any thing unto him: for now I know that thou fearest God, seeing thou hast not withheld thy son, thine only son from me."*

There comes another word from God that is a proceeding word, and Abraham is saying, now wait a minute God, you just told me to sacrifice him. Abraham now has to obey his proceeding word and stay his hand and not lay his hand upon the lad.

Isaac has a part in this too. Because he was not a very young child, as some had thought. He was older and he had to get on the altar himself. He could have refused, but he did not. God needed a father in the earth that was willing to sacrifice his son and a son that was willing to be sacrificed. Their obedience was needed in order for God to have access to the earth. That is another lesson, but I want you to get what is happening with this proceeding word. Look at what Isaac asked his father ("Where is the lamb for a burnt offering")? And the reply that Abraham gave him ("God will provide...").

> *"And Isaac spake unto Abraham his father, and said, My father: and he said, Here am I, my son. And he said, Behold the fire and the wood: but where is the lamb for a burnt offering? 8 And Abraham said, My son, God will provide himself a lamb for a burnt offering: so they went both of them together."* Genesis 22:7-8

There are times when you have to say some things in Greek, Hebrew, Jehovah Jireh (God will provide), or whatever other language you have to use, to make sure that you say the right thing. Abraham would have followed through with the preceding word (and he would have had a dead promise); but he had to obey God and be in full agreement with that preceding word, before he got the proceeding word.

Remember what Jesus said, that we should live by his proceeding word – **Matt. 4:4: "...It is written, Man shall not live by bread alone, but by every word that proceedeth out of the mouth of God."** Many times God tries us in our hearing. How obedient are we going to be, according to what God says?

Know Who You Are Called To Serve

Remember Elijah place of purpose in 1 Kings 17. He had a deeper purpose. It was to become somebody's man of purpose, and it was the widow woman, and now his hearing had to be tested again. We see that in *1* Kings 17:7-16:

"And it came to pass after a while, that the brook dried up, because there had been no rain in the land. 8 And the word of the LORD came unto him, saying, 9 Arise, get thee to Zarephath, which belongeth to Zidon, and dwell there: behold, I have commanded a widow woman there to sustain thee. 10 So he arose and went to Zarephath. And when he came to the gate of the city, behold, the widow woman was there gathering of sticks: and he called to her, and said, Fetch me, I pray thee, a little water in a vessel, that I may drink. 11 And as she was going to fetch it, he called to her, and said, Bring me, I pray thee, a morsel of bread in thine hand. 12 And she said, As the LORD thy God liveth, I have not a cake, but an handful of meal in a barrel, and a little oil in a cruse: and, behold, I am gathering two sticks, that I may go in and dress it for me and my son, that we may eat it, and die. 13 And Elijah said unto her, Fear not; go and do as thou hast said: but make me thereof a little cake first, and bring it unto me, and after make for thee and for thy son. 14 For thus saith the LORD God of Israel, The barrel of meal shall not waste, neither shall the cruse of oil fail, until the day that the LORD sendeth rain upon the earth. 15 And she went and did according to the saying of Elijah: and she, and he, and her house, did eat many days. 16 And

the barrel of meal wasted not, neither did the cruse of oil fail, according to the word of the LORD, which he spake by Elijah."

God had to test his hearing again. Because now he has to go to another place called "there," and when he goes to Zarephath, he does not get a physical confirmation, because that woman is planning to die. Therefore, you are not going to get a confirmation, you have to proceed strictly on what God said, and that has to be enough.

I love this but I did not love it, when I was going through it. I had no physical proof, but I still heard God and there was a sensing to go ahead and obey that, and I would say "God I don't see any confirmation on what you told me." And God said, "Rodney, at this next level, you don't get physical confirmation. You are a prophet and you don't need a confirmation." You are the voice of God, you do not need a confirmation, and you heard God. You heard God and the thing that God is trying to do now, is to get us to grow up. As a lamb or sheep, God will grant you a confirmation, but once you start to grow in the prophetic, you don't need a confirmation. Let's look at this in 2 Cor. 12:1-5:

"It is not expedient for me doubtless to glory. I will come to visions and revelations of the Lord. 2 I knew a man in Christ above fourteen years ago, (whether in the body, I cannot tell; or whether out of the body, I cannot tell: God knoweth;) such an one caught up to the third heaven. 3 And I knew such a man, (whether in the body, or out of the body, I cannot tell: God knoweth;) 4 How that he was caught up into paradise, and heard unspeakable words, which it is not lawful for a man to utter. 5 Of such an one will I glory: yet of myself I will not glory, but in mine infirmities."   *2 Corinthians 12:1-5*

Paul is seeing some things here; he is no longer in the lamb or sheep stage. He has graduated to Apostle status but he still wants to revert back to the old way of doing things. He is in the earth trying to explain what he is seeing in heaven. He could not explain it, because he is speaking unspeakable words in our world. That was the old way of doing things. We do that too by trying to explain things to people that we are not called to explain. They don't understand what we are saying, because we are saying unspeakable words in their world. We are not crazy they just cannot understand what we are saying. Let's look a little further at what Paul is saying:

> *"For though I would desire to glory, I shall not be a fool; for I will say the truth: but now I forbear, lest any man should think of me above that which he seeth me to be, or that he heareth of me. 7 And lest I should be exalted above measure through the abundance of the revelations, there was given to me a thorn in the flesh, the messenger of Satan to buffet me, lest I should be exalted above measure."*
> *2 Corinthians 12:6-7*

God did not give Paul a messenger of Satan. What you sow to your flesh, you are going to reap to your flesh; and what you sow to your spirit, you will reap in your spirit. Paul wants God to take the messenger of Satan from him. So, he asked God three times to take it away, because that was what Paul was used to doing, to get rid of things. Like us, he went to where he was comfortable. Take a look at what Paul said to Jesus and what Jesus said back to him in 2 Cor. "12:8-9

> *"For this thing I besought the Lord thrice, that it might depart from me. 9 And he said unto me, My grace is sufficient for thee: for my strength is made perfect in weakness. Most gladly therefore will I rather glory in my infirmities, that the power of Christ may rest upon me."*
> *2 Corinthians 12:8-9*

I am talking to Prophets and prophetic people, there comes a time when you must grow up, far beyond what you are used to. Here we see an Apostle talking about asking God three times to get this thing off of him; but Jesus said, "My grace is sufficient for thee." Jesus was not talking about His saving grace, this is an empowering substance.

Know Who You Are Called To Serve Under

This is the reason that you have to know who you are called to serve under, because it is their grace that you will receive. I personally cannot serve under weak leadership. I need to know that you can handle some things. The Apostle Paul is now walking under the leadership of Jesus Christ, and Paul is under His grace. There is a strong prophetic grace on the church that I pastor, and it is not strange for people to prophecy, because of that prophetic grace. When you do the thing that connects you to the grace, it will rest on you. Remember, we talked about you deciding to do something earlier. You can do that, if you buy into the grace of that. God is saying to us, you take the shotgun, now that you are of age. He is not going to do it for you anymore. I had to decide that I wanted to hear like my man of God was hearing. I bought into what they were saying. I believe that my man and woman of God were hearing God. If I went off course, it would be because they went off course, and God would have to deal with them, because I bought into what they were saying. So if I went off course, God would come and get me, before I went off the cliff.

How bad do you want to hear God? One time God told me to go in a trash can because He wanted me to get something out of there. I found a book on finances that I wanted, but I did not have the resources to purchase the book. Now pride gets in the way sometimes, but I had to obey God. There were other times that God told me to look in the trash and I didn't find anything, or at least I did not go down far enough in the trash to find what God was talking about, but I knew that it was God.

NOTE

CHAPTER 8

The Prophet's Mantle (The Gift of Access)

There are certain keys that unlock the mantle of the prophet and in this class you will learn twelve of those keys that we have never released in any class before now. This new class material every prophet must learn or continue to walk without the three principles that cause the release of power.

We must understand that there are various mantles in various areas of leadership. If one desired the mantle of their leader they had to understand and learn to walk in the three principles for functioning that causes a release on them of the same power, grace and anointing that rests on your leader/father.

Wearing the mantle is common for the person that serves as the successor of the leader/father. It would not be incorrect to call this the "Mantle of Succession". The successor knows how to effectively handle the leader's mantle just as they learned how to handle their leader. If you don't know how to handle the leader you will not know how to handle his mantle. Let's look at the three principles:

Principle #1 <u>Succession</u>: You can be a successor like Joshua and Elisha were and receive the mantle of your leader or you can follow the example of Jehaziel, Elisha's servant who failed to receive the mantle due to greed operating in his heart. The principle of succession is simple: as you walk under the hand of your leader and serve well, his mantle comes on you. We find that Elisha served well and got double of what was on his leader. By his example, we will see that there are some things he did that stands out:

- *He refused to listen to other voices around him.*
- *He served closer than anyone else around him.*
- *He served without quitting and was given reason to do so by Elijah.*
- *He created an unwavering focus on purpose.*
- *He stayed in proper and prophetic alignment with his leader.*

Principle #2 <u>Serving Well</u>: Every leader that serves well captures the spirit of his leader. Many people will never receive their leader's spirit because they fail at the serving level. Serving opens up your leader's heart towards you when ordinarily his heart would not have opened. Why not? You must realize that your leader sees and serves many people, yet feels all alone when it is time to accomplish the assignment or when he is pouring out and there is no evidence that those following him are receiving. When *your heart opens to help him his heart does likewise in releasing to you.*

Principle #3: <u>Submission</u>: Submission is defined as (1) a willingness to yield or surrender to somebody, or the act of doing so or (2) demanded nothing less than total submission to someone in authority.

<u>*What Is A Mantle?*</u>

A Mantle is a loose-fitting garment worn by prophets and other officials in authority to signify their position and power to exercise dominion. Mantles reflect latitude, stature, prestige, and provisions of the wearer, as well as the license to act.

We must understand how a mantle operates for a prophet for the power and authority of a prophet lies in the mantle. The mantle is designed to keep you going, providing protection in the most adverse conditions. Just as Elisha upon receiving the mantle used it to cross back over the Jordan River, the mantle is designed to cause break-through for you when used properly. Had he not carefully observed Elijah create a crossing point of dry land in the midst of the Jordan, Elisha would not have known how to use the mantle to get back over the Jordan. His ability to strike the river with the mantle to cross it resulted from him purposing to remain close to his leader and to observe what he did. Otherwise Elisha would have been stuck on the wrong side of the river and would not have been delivered.

As a Successor you have to have the same heart for the assignment your leader has. If your leader has a heart for intercession you have to embrace that as well. If your leader has a heart for the prophetic you have to embrace that as well. Often times you have to be the runner or the mediator, the one who serves as the go between.

> *"Therefore turn thou to thy God: keep mercy and judgment, and wait on thy God continually –"* Hosea 12:6.

As we look at the setting of this verse in Hosea 12:1-6, we find both the Nation of Judah and the Nation of Israel in a backslidden condition and God calling the people back to repentance and fellowship with Him. We can use as an example, Jacob who struggled with God to make it back to a place of favor in Him. It is important to see who God called to this place of intercession for the people. God calls for the Prophet as one to intercede for and speak prophetically to the people. God would also call for the Prophet to prophesy the people into destiny, and before doing so, the seer/intercessor comes to break up fallow ground. But it must be understood that the intercessor at this time may be called to the prophet's side. They both will come to melt the hearts of the hardhearted and also to clear the atmosphere of hindrances. This kind of word is easily received once the seer/intercessor has done their job. God is saying return! Now understanding that the prophet is on assignment and so is the intercessor, the thing we should see is that the mantle of the prophet could come on the intercessor or successor at this time of serving the prophet. Both the intercessor and successor that serves the prophet must know how to treat the vestments of the prophet.

Mantle Treatment is defined as that which is learned, practiced, supplied to, and provided for within the mantle of ministers in order to equip and empower them for service to the Lord. These treatments are beyond normal church attendance and believer's Bible studies. Mentorship, schools of ministry (especially for the prophet and the apostle), and ministry apprenticeship are needed for effective treatment of one's mantle. These preparations are usually above what the typical Christian receives or is exposed to in church services. Their distinction is that these treatments help ministers serve more competently and confidently in the execution of their assigned posts.

Keep mercy and judgment

Mercy is the place of mediation; a place of intercession; and where we prefer others above ourselves. This is where principle number three is enforced. The successor at this point is not going according to what he thinks but according to what the prophet knows. Although neither of them are mercy driven, God powerfully moves through them in prophetic intercession, revealing His mind and His purpose to them. Remember the prophet is doing what is in the mind of God and the successor is doing what is in the mind of the prophet. While the prophet intercedes and is being sensitized to what God desires to happen, they are under strict orders not to speak but to pray as an intercessor. It is at this time of sensitivity and intimacy that the successor gets into the heart of the prophet. Remember the word "assignment". As the prophet shifts into his assignment the assignment of the successor shifts and he comes closer to the mantle.

> *"Let us therefore come boldly unto the throne of grace, that we may obtain mercy and find grace to help in time of need."* Hebrew 4:16

*So here we come into intercession with a real sense of dying to who we are, and to who we think we are, as we become aware of our place of intercession or the place of assignment. In a counseling session, you don't look to say much for yourself. Look at this as **inter – session**. You enter a session to make something happen for someone else. We violate the whole principle of succession when we don't learn to enter a session on someone else's behalf. This is a learned art that is a powerful principle of succession. We are using intercession as an example but I think you are really getting it. This is going to teach you how to embrace the heart of your leader.*

Place of judgment

Judgment is truth, coming back to a place of divine order, keeping His council, and being obedient to His laws. The place of judgment is the place of "prophetic influence". The very heart of the Father is mercy and the very heart of the prophet is results. When we understand the heart of the leader we get closer to the mantle. Let's take the word HEART -- if we remove the H and T (H**EAR**T) we come up with the word **EAR**. In order to effectively intercede you must be able to hear. Once this has been accomplished, remove the H and E (HE**ART**) and we come up with the word **ART**. Intercession is seeking the heart of the Father while using the art to make one free.

The prophetic influence is when we have the mind of the Spirit and are able to communicate the very purpose of our God. If we are going to wait on God continually by keeping mercy, remaining in the place of prophetic influence, then God is going to have to become our top priority and in many cases our only priority! As a prophet we are called to keep order, keep judgment, and keep mercy. Keep in mind that when Jonah showed up in the city of Ninevah, he kept judgment as well as divine order. Jonah stated that in forty days God would pour out His wrath and judgment on the city. However, when the people of Ninevah repented Jonah did not remember mercy. The goal of the prophet is to speak and pray that God will have mercy! Instead of praying for mercy, most of us would rather see wrath because we have failed to maintain that place of mercy. Keep in mind that the sign of a great prophet is to speak and have it come to pass. Also, the sign of an even greater prophet is one who lives in the place of intercession, speaks and has it not to come to pass, because God has averted it. Why? Because of His mercy! God must keep judgment and order, but He rather keeps mercy. If people will hear His divine order, recognize the error of their way, and repent, then God will be swift to remember mercy. Notice which comes first – keep mercy and keep judgment.

"That this is a rebellious people, lying children, children that will not hear the law of the Lord. Which say to the seers, see not; not unto us right things, speak unto us smooth things, prophesy deceits: Get you out of the way, turn aside out of the path, cause the Holy One of Israel to cease from before us." Isaiah 30:9-11

This is clearly people that have had their heart seared as with a hot iron. Their hearts are calloused. Remember all the things that happen when one's heart is affected or infected.

Keep judgment

Adhere to the command and instructions of God coming out of the mouth of His prophets. The rebellious people rejected and refused the prophetic influence of their God and the discipline it would bring. The prophetic speaks of the divine inspiration, divine illumination, divine revelation, divine activation, divine participation, divine intervention, and divine involvement. To reject the prophetic voice or influence of God is to reject God's active involvement. God wants to be actively involved with His people.

God will raise up individuals in the midst of the assembly, having the prophetic mantle upon them, having the prophetic voice, and lifting up the horn. "Lifting up the horn" is a term used to describe those who function and operate in the prophetic in some way, shape, or form. Prophetic and intercessory hearing stems out of the heart. It is so very important that your heart be clean and pure. No prophet, seer, or intercessor can operate with a clouded or closed heart.

"Moreover, David and the captains of the host separated to the service of the sons of Asaph, and of Heman, and of Jeduthun, who should prophesy with harps, with psalteries, and with cymbals: and the number of the workmen according to their service."
I Chronicles 25:1

"All of these were the sons of Heman the king's seer in the words of God, to lift up the horn. And God gave to Heman fourteen sons and three daughters."
I Chronicles 25:5

If the prophet, seer and intercessor would hear and obey, they would become a prophetic voice clothed with the same prophetic anointing while speaking the same prophetic message. Why doesn't the church have the prophetic mantle on it? The mantle is a type of vestment that is reserved for the office of the prophet. Therefore, one receives the mantle and the other receives an anointing that flows off of the mantle.

The church is called to be God's prophetic voice in this dark world. Remember that the seer is called to work in connection with the leader. The prophet is to be God's prophetic voice and prophetic influence in the earth. Yet the church is to be an anointed prophetic vehicle that will greatly influence the earth. God has not only set aside a specialized group called a prophetic people, but through the Spirit of Prophesy, God desires to use the entire church to be a prophetic influence in the earth. The purpose of the church is to lift up the horn.

> *"And I fell at his feet to worship Him. And he said unto me, see thou do it not: I am thy fellow servant, and of thy brethren that have the testimony of Jesus: worship God: for the testimony of Jesus is the spirit of prophecy."*   Revelation 19:10

Through and by this spirit of prophecy, God desires to use the church to bring change in the life of the world. This is where the anointing to prophesy will come on a spirit filled vessel. The important issue is that we remember that this is still not the seer/intercessor.

"And the Lord came down in a cloud, and spake unto him, and took up the spirit that was upon him, and gave it unto the seventy elders; and it came to pass that when the spirit rested upon them, they prophesied, and did not cease. ... And Moses said unto him, enviest thou for my sake? Would God that all the Lord's people were prophets, and that the Lord would put his spirit upon them."
Numbers 11:24-29

There is a great anointing available to all those that are like-minded, or of the same blood type. The same blood type is important if there is to be a continual flow of the prophetic or the anointing of the intercessor. The church is God's vehicle of His divine presence. We are the vessels or channels of and for His divine flow in the earth. The church is called to act as one man, function as one man, and flow as one man. A prophetic people are those who have a prophetic anointing on them for service. They don't have it on them at all times, yet when the anointing does come on them, it is for service. In order for you and I to wait on God, continually staying under the anointing, we must remain at the place of mediation/intercession and the place of prophetic influence. Just as you have a right and left hand, you have the gift of intercession and a prophetic anointing on you, if you are a seer. To operate in one without the other as a seer, is to operate using only one hand. To operate in the prophetic without being an intercessor is to operate using only one hand.

It is important to understand that intercession is closely tied to the position of the seer and the source of the prophetic power is found at that place of intimacy with their father. It behooves us to keep in mind that before we can have or release power for God in the prophetic in a public forum, we must first receive power with God in that place of worship and intimacy in the private setting. The greater the prophet is at the place of worship and fellowship with the Father, Son and Holy Spirit, the greater the impact the prophet will make when operating in the prophetic.

The greater the seer is in the place of intercession, the greater they will be in the prophetic flow. Remember the prophetic flow of the seer is in their seeing and not in speaking. To whom much is given in prophetic seeing, much is required in the place of intercession. There must be a deposit that will come out of us according to the investment made in us.

"And when thou prayest, thou shalt not be as the hypocrites are: for they love to pray standing in the synagogues and in the corners of the streets, that they may be seen of men. Verily I say unto you, they have their reward. But thou, when thou prayest, enter into thy closet, and when thou hast shut thy door, pray to the Father which is in secret; and thy Father which seeth in secret shall reward thee openly."
Matthew 6:5-6

Now in the case where God will choose to use a tag team knowingly or unknowingly, one will do most of the intercession and the other will do most of the prophesying. We have to keep in mind that much of our prophesying is simply the reaping of the anointing from our covering.

There is a great flowing of the anointing off of the prophet, down on the seer. The place of intercession is the sowing, and the operating in the prophetic in a public setting is the reaping. We must remain humble as a prophetic people and as a seeing/intercessory people, because unless we are given to the place of intercession as well, someone else is doing most of the dirty work for us. We who are used by

God in the prophetic are used to gain the increase of God. God has given us seed to sow yet except we go to the field or the place of sowing there will not be a harvest. Always keep in mind the price that the intercessor had to pay before God would ever allow that word to be given or deliverance to be realized. Everybody wants to be the one that God will use to give the word that brings deliverance but very few are willing to be used by God to be the one who would pay the price for it. Remember the word declare that "many are called but few are chosen". There is a reason that God would say that to the body of Christ, and especially to a body of seers/intercessors. There is an investment that must come out of your inner man. It is more than a price – it is an investment. Before there is a smell of fragrance there must come a breaking or a crushing first. The intercessor, seer, and the prophetic person pay their price in a type of "Garden of Gethsemane" (place of crushing). The fragrance or rejoicing can take place now that you have sown or invested yourself in the kingdom.

"And he that reapeth receiveth wages, and gathereth fruit unto life eternal: that both he that soweth and he that reapeth may rejoice together. And herein is that saying true, one soweth, and another reapeth. I sent you to reap that whereon ye bestowed no labour: other men laboured, and ye are entered into their labours." John 4:36-38

The key to the power of God that is released in the prophetic is found in the place of intimacy with God through worship. Out of what you see through the flow of personal worship prophetic intercession is provoked. In the place of personal worship you see the heart of God in a different way. After knowing the endlessness of His grace, you will also come to know the passion that God has for souls and their next place in God. Not only will you come to know that part of God, you will also come to know His endless grace which surpasses the understanding of man. It is not the will of God that any should perish but that all should come to repentance. This is where the art and the power of prophetic worship and intercession come into play.

The power is not in the mechanics of what you do when you prophesy, but it is in the life force behind your prophesying. We want you to not only know how to prophesy, but we also want you to understand the gifts that operate within the prophetic. Yes, it is important to understand the gifts and how to operate in the prophetic, but the problem with most of us is we are only concerned with the mechanics, and not the spirit of life that is suppose to back up what we are doing. There is a form or formula to the approach of the mechanics of our prophesying, but this in operation alone denies the power. Please remember that there is no one, two, or three steps to prophesying, but there is a one step approach and principle to abide by. The one step approach is the step up into intimacy. Intimacy causes a birthing of the breath of God. You can't have intimacy without worship. It is worship that provokes the prophetic flow. If we say we want the power of God manifested in our lives, yet we never get into a place of worship, we are actually denying the power.

"For men shall be lovers of their own selves, ... Lovers of pleasures more than lovers of God. Having a form of godliness, but denying the power thereof; from such turn away. ... Ever learning, and never able to come to the knowledge of the truth." II Timothy 3:1-7

*Jesus said that what we do privately God will reward openly. Now the danger is when we fail to understand that the prophetic gift is a grace gift. The grace gifts can be used by God anytime and anywhere. All that has to happen is for the anointing to flow and that gift will turn on and we will begin to reap where we have applied ourselves. This is called grace gifts because of the empowerment of those gifts. This is prophetic gifting and **not** the Office of the Prophet. Always keep in mind that the gifts of the Spirit are grace gifts and not fruit, which have to be developed over time, pain, patience, and pressure. Even though there is no need for the gifts themselves to be developed there is a need for you as the user to be developed before using them. God may use you powerfully in the prophetic gifts but you are only reaping where you have applied yourself. If you have not applied yourself to be used in the area of these gifts, God will not choose you when it is time for the gift to work. Many of us walk around in spiritual pride because of the prophetic gift that has been turned on, but really we have done nothing to earn it. Intercession will sometime precede the prophetic. Someone occasionally had to pay the price in private if someone else will be used in public. Everyone wants the public life, being seen of men, but very few choose the private life before the Father. The secret to God's power is the private life of preparation, what we do before God and Him alone. It is what we do behind closed doors that count. God will send His power, and honor the vessel that Honors him.*

We can't honor Him publicly unless we first honor Him privately. We as prophets, prophetic people, and seers/ intercessors are measured by what we do privately first, not by what we do publicly. God will measure us first in the secret place, not in the place of the open forum. Can you imagine the power that will be released openly when we speak that prophetic utterance, if the power is first released out of our mouth privately in the place of worship and the intercessor shaking the atmosphere in their private place. If we can keep our hearts right before God, constantly in fellowship with Him, staying in that place of prayer and intercession, there will never be a problem with God using us.

"And Jesus answered them saying, the hour is come, that the son of man should be glorified. Verily, verily I say unto you, except a corn of wheat fall into the ground and die, it abideth alone: but if it die, it bringeth forth much fruit. He that loveth this life shall lose it; and he that hateth his life in this world shall keep it unto life eternal. If any man serve me, let him follow me; and where I am, there shall also my servant be: if any man serve me, him will my Father honor." John 12:23-26

NOTE

Cycles of Apostolic Reproduction

I t is imperative that we progress as people that are going

to be productive. It is important that we understand the process of development where we are functioning according to purpose. We are going to look at the development of the Apostles' in order to take hold of and identify those things that God has handpicked us to operate in so that we begin to function according to the way that God has created us. What is the reason that you are on the earth? Why do you exist? We need to understand why we are here on earth. To accomplish this I want to talk about cycles of Apostolic Reproduction.

The word "Apostolic" comes from the word Apostle, which means "one sent". When we think about the first Church, remember that Jesus wants to make sure that you and I serve the purpose that we came to serve. Therefore, it becomes imperative that we understand why we are here. One of the reasons that I believe some people do not come into their purpose is because they never make the right hookup so that they can develop into who God intended them to be.

Let's take a look at Matthew 16 so that we will be able to find our place in the body of Christ.

"When Jesus came into the coasts of Caesarea Philippi, he asked his disciples, saying, Whom do men say that I the Son of man am? 14 And they said, Some say that thou art John the Baptist: some, Elias; and others, Jeremias, or one of the prophets. 15 He saith unto them, But whom say ye that I am? 16 And Simon Peter answered and said, Thou art the Christ, the Son of the living God. 17 And Jesus answered and said unto him, Blessed art thou, Simon Barjona: for flesh and blood hath not revealed it unto thee, but my Father which is in heaven. 18 And I say also unto thee, That thou art Peter, and upon this rock I will build my church; and the gates of hell shall not prevail against it. 19 And I will give unto thee the keys of the kingdom of heaven: and whatsoever thou shalt bind on earth shall be bound in heaven: and whatsoever thou shalt loose on earth shall be loosed in heaven. 20 Then charged he his disciples that they should tell no man that he was Jesus the Christ."   Matthew 16:13-20 13

Through this process Jesus was training twelve disciples who later became the twelve Apostles. From these Apostles, he developed the entire church as we know it today. Through this overall process the entire body of Christ was developed so that we could serve our purpose. Jesus wanted to make sure that you and I serve our purpose and that we be developed into whom God intended us to be.

Peter recognized Jesus for who He was saying; ***"Thou art the Christ, the Son of the living God"*** and Jesus begins to say ***"Blessed art thou, Simon Barjona: for flesh and blood hath not revealed it unto thee, but my Father which is in heaven. 18 And I say also unto thee, that thou art Peter, and upon this rock I will build my church; and the gates of hell shall not prevail against it"***. The gates of hell are not supposed to prevail against us because it is to us, the church, that Jesus gave the power so that we would really walk in that power and dominion so that we would subdue those things that need to be subdued on this planet.

Apostolic Reproduction is something that God wants us to do so that we are developed as we need to be developed. It takes place through the process of spiritual fathering with son reception. This process is the giver-receiver principle. I can give, but if there is no receiver, nothing can really happen because there is no receiver in the earth that is receiving what was intended.

Apostolic Reproduction is a six point process: Recognition, Reception, Reproduction, Replication, Releasing and Reigning. The completion of the process is to reign - to subdue and have dominion. Remember, we have to make sure that we are developed in the area that we need to be developed. Whatever that area is we need to dominate that area. One of the things that we need to look at first is the six point process.

Let's look at *1 Kings 19:15-16, 19:*

"And the LORD said unto him, Go, return on thy way to the wilderness of Damascus: and when thou comest, anoint Hazael to be king over Syria: 16 And Jehu the son of Nimshi shalt thou anoint to be king over Israel: and Elisha the son of Shaphat of Abel-meholah shalt thou anoint to be prophet in thy room. 19 So he departed thence, and found Elisha the son of Shaphat, who was plowing with twelve yoke of oxen before him, and he with the twelfth: and Elijah passed by him, and cast his mantle upon him." 1 Kings 19:15-16, 19

Here you have a man called Elisha moving about in the earth minding his father's business and God selects him to do this job. This is just like you and I working on our secular job or business not realizing that God's has a purpose for us. Many of us may get overlooked because we are not being faithful with the things that belong to our father. In this passage we are talking about Elisha's biological father. Elijah comes along to anoint Elisha in his place. Now Elisha is going to have to go through his development process or his training process in order to come into this. If you are ever going to come to the place in life where you function according to purpose, you must be developed from the inside out.

RECOGNITION

Recognition is the first step in the process. You have to be at a place of recognition before you are ever recognized. Looking at this passage, we realize that Elisha was doing something before he was recognized. One of the things that I share with people who are believing God for their God mate, the person that God intended for them to have is "You need to find yourself doing the will of God," otherwise the wrong someone is going to find you. And then when you are in church, they are not going to be with you because that is not where you found them. When you found them they were not in the will of God. While you are single you need to make sure that you are doing the will of God so you can be recognized. We want to be recognized by the one who is designed to move us into purpose because God always assigns someone to do that. Elisha is doing exactly what he was supposed to do. He was faithful taking care of his father's business and that is how he got recognized. This is the place of recognition.

Elijah was recognized because he was doing what he was supposed to be doing in that season. God told Elijah to go and anoint Elisha in his room because he is faithful handling his father's business; he is faithful doing his job. Now you say "How do I get recognized?" If you have not come to the season of recognition, you should be doing whatever your hands find to do. You are not always going to be doing what you are called to do in that season, so you need to be doing what your leader is asking you to do. Some of us get so spiritual and want to ask if the Lord wants us to do this. Did your pastor ask you? If he did, then the Lord wants you to do it.

Let's check that out in John 2:1-4:

> *" And the third day there was a marriage in Cana of Galilee; and the mother of Jesus was there: 2 And both Jesus was called, and his disciples, to the marriage. 3 And when they wanted wine, the mother of Jesus saith unto him, They have no wine. 4 Jesus saith unto her, Woman, what have I to do with thee? mine hour is not yet come.*

We see that it was clearly not Jesus' time to do miracles, but He did what his authority in the earth asked Him to do. Mary was the woman of authority here. Jesus told His mother that it was not his time to be recognized. Is this the will of God? Did God want Him to do what she asked? Did He do it? Yes! Why, because He was asked by His authoritative figure in the earth. Mary understood that it was not His time, but she let Him know that this is what we need right now. So it was the will of God to do what she needed to have done at that time. Elisha was not called to walk behind oxen, but that was what his father needed him to do.

RECEPTION

The sons must be receptive to the father. An example of not receiving fathering is refusing to obey the order of the house. If the order of the house is that the usher seat everyone according to a particular plan and the leader has sanctioned the plan. The usher is under the authority of the father. Sons that are not receiving will not sit where the ushers tell them to sit. Since they know that their father has requested that the ushers make sure that certain seats are filled and if they refuse to sit where the ushers assign them, they are not receiving and are not being effectively fathered. The fathering is being given out, but are you receptive?

Let's go to John because I want you to see Jesus doing the same thing that God did. In this passage, Jesus had been raised from the dead; his time was almost over and none of the disciples are recognized. So you say what was Jesus doing all of this time? He was forming and shaping the disciples. He was putting them together, making sure that they had word in them. He was rebuking them and making sure that they were coming into an image that He could be pleased to flow into, but they don't have any breath in them yet. *"Then said Jesus to them again, Peace be unto you: as my Father hath sent me, even so send I you." (John 20:21-22)* None of them were recognized at this time, but they had taken on the form and shape that they needed and were ready to be breathed in.

Some of you are not ready to be breathed on because you have not taken on any form or shape. Why? One of the reasons is that you have yet been fathered. Fathering gives you shape and cause you to look like someone. Who do you look like? You look like who is fathering you. You are going to take on their image and become what they are saying. This is one of the reasons that you should watch your leader like a hawk because you are getting an image. You check out how he gets the word. Then you need to make sure that you are getting the word. You also need to check his fasting life and then you need to take that on. Identify what is he talking about and once you find out, take that on. Once you do this, you begin to come to the place of being transformed. What does my leader think about music or doctrine? All of this is giving me some form. What does your father think about whatever subject that comes into your heart? Because these subjects are in your heart, you need some answers so that you can get some form to those things.

Let's think about some of the things that Jesus' disciples asked Him. One was Lord teach us how to pray as John has taught his disciples to pray! Lord what about fasting? Do we really need to fast? Lord what about eating with unwashed hands? Does that really matter? Am I going to hell because my hands are dirty? Talk to us about the end time; Lord what is going to happen in the end time? From all of this they are taking on a form.

When you are in the reception process, you are engaged in spiritual impartation from your father (male or female) over time. During this time there was relationship and impartation, relationship and more impartation. Remember that there was a ten year period between Elisha's recognition and reception. You are engaged in relationship.

This is the time to ask your leader questions. This is your time of formation.

Look at verse 21 again; *"Then said Jesus to them again, Peace be unto you: as my Father hath sent me, even so send I you."* Jesus is telling them here that the same way my Father sent me, I am sending you. Now what is a sent one? An Apostle! So now an Apostle is one of the five-fold calls. The Apostle is one sent. So Jesus is literally saying; the same way I am an Apostle in the earth, that is what you are and this is the form that you should be taking. Now Jesus is breathing on them what He is. We see that in verse 22: *"And when he had said this, he breathed on them, and saith unto them, Receive ye the Holy Ghost:"* In other words, He is saying receive the Spirit that is on Me. He breathed on them and said receive my Spirit. When He breathed on them, the Holy Spirit which was on Him came on them. We see from this that they were being fathered.

Remember in Genesis 2:7 God creates man and blows everything that He is in him. He inhales and exhales everything that He is in man, He put Himself in us. That is one of the reasons why Jesus said in Matt 5:48: *"Be ye therefore perfect , even as your Father which is in heaven is perfect."* God expects us to be perfect because of what He put in us.

Two Elements of Receiving

There are two elements for this process: one of them is _transference, which means transferring your spirit as God did on the behalf of Moses with the elders Moses selected._

"And the LORD said unto Moses, Gather unto me seventy men of the elders of Israel, whom thou knowest to be the elders of the people, and officers over them; and bring them unto the tabernacle of the congregation, that they may stand there with thee." (Num 11:16-17, 25) Moses had to select those that he knew to be elders of the people. This is the reason that you should watch who you receive a word from because they do not really know you. You need to know your man or woman of God and they should also know you. They get to know you because you are coming to Sunday Service and Bible Study. Now if someone other than your spiritual father gives you a word, you can be nice or courteous, but do not bank on that word because they may give you that word out of season. However, you man or woman of God knows you and they will not give you a word too soon. God asked Moses, "Do you know 70 that are mature, that know wisdom because I want to breathe on them and put your spirit on them. Then they were able to do what Moses did. They were able to help Moses bear the burdens of the people.

" And I will come down and talk with thee there: and I will take of the spirit which is upon thee, and will put it upon them; and they shall bear the burden of the people with thee, that thou bear it not thyself alone."   *Numbers 11:16-17*

"And the LORD came down in a cloud, and spake unto him, and took of the spirit that was upon him, and gave it unto the seventy elders: and it came to pass, that, when the spirit rested upon them, they prophesied, and did not cease."   *Numbers 11:25*

Remember transference means to transfer the spirit on one person to another person the same way that God took the spirit off of Moses and put it on those he selected. You should receive from your father, his spirit and not from others. Some of those others have the wrong spirit on them and you can get a wrong spirit on you if you receive that. When Moses' elders received his spirit, they prophesied and did not cease. I don't recall that Moses did a lot of prophesying but it was in him and it was in him by virtue of his spirit and all they had to do was to take on the form of his image. Once they received his spirit, they had access to that and they started doing the works of Moses.

I am a prophet and those that are submitted to me and come to Sunday and mid-week service week after week should feel prophecy boiling up on the inside of them because it is on me. Those that have my spirit will experience this. No matter what your part is, you want to prophecy even if your part is singing. Sometimes you just want to speak a word of prophecy through your song. Why? Because God will take of the spirit, the anointing or the oil that rests on me and put it on you even if you don't know that He is doing that. Now I will know that He is doing that because that is a part of the process. God will just do that because you are being faithful. He will put on someone else because they are being faithful. They get a transfer.

The process of being selected to receive from your father takes time. It may take eight to ten years for one of my sons to get my spirit on them. It was ten years from the time of recognition to the reception of Elijah's spirit on Elisha. If my calculation is correct I am just getting my spiritual father's spirit on me. I do not believe that I am too far from that because he can correct me and I am fine with that. I do not get an attitude or walk off from him because he corrected me. I am not just going to walk out and be a wanderer. I know people right now that are supposed to be where God has set them but they are wanderers. If God is in it, you should connect with the place where God is sending you before you leave where you are now. "Am I in the right place?" is the last thing you should be thinking if you connected with where you are going before you get there. It is a matter of leaving and cleaving. You need to do this because you need to have the spirit of your father on you.

The second of the two key elements is *impartation*. *Impartation is the reception of communication of information or knowledge of a particular quality.*

Impartation causes the following four conditions:

- *Separation (evaluating relationship),*
- *Connection (Leaving and Cleaving),*
- *Declaration (say who you are with) and*
- *Manifestation (Demonstrate)*

Impartation happens even if you don't know it. You just know that something happens to you on Sunday when the word is going forth. You don't leave the way you came. You leave with peace or joy or something wonderful that you did not come with.

Separation

Impartation will cause separation to take place when you start evaluating your relationships. Now that you are getting word on another level, it starts to expose information about the people that you fellowship with. The word starts to expose them for who they are. At first you had the wrong spirit on you and you felt alright to be with them. You knew that they were not right and nothing around them was right, but you felt that is was alright to be with them because you had the wrong spirit on you. But then the word that you were getting in you started to shed light on the relationship and you started to think that this may not be what I need to be a part of. All of a sudden, it was not alright to be around them and so a separation takes place. But the separation never comes without you making another connection -a leaving and cleaving.

Connection
You have to leave something to cleave to something else. You cannot be faithful in more than one place. So you leave somewhere so that you could cleave somewhere else. You have to really connect to the point of weaving together our minds. For example, I have a problem when members refer to the church that I pastor as only "my" church. When you start connecting with the church, it is not my church it is "our" church. Those are not just my people, but they are our people. If you feel the need to say "your" people, you are not completely connected. You have to really get connected to make sure that there is no static in your line and lay ownership to what we are called to do. When you completely connect, the anointing that is on us starts to come on you and you start to enjoy the same anointing.

We have to really connect properly. That means that we have to leave and cleave. Remember your spirit is too important to let just anybody speak to it. Words are spirit and they are life. Jesus said this in *John 6:63:* " *... words that I speak unto you, they are spirit, and they are life.* " Now if I am listening to someone that is not hooked up with my father in any kind of a way there is not much that is going to be said that is not contrary to what my father is saying. Therefore, I have to be careful not to get the wrong stuff in me. I need to make sure that this is a God given word to me. I need to know that what I am getting is from God for me. One of my gripes with community choirs is that they have strange fire. God spoke to Moses about this concerning two of Aaron's sons who did what they were not authorized to do in Lev 10:1: *"And Nadab and Abihu, the sons of Aaron, took either of them his censer, and put fire therein, and put incense thereon, and offered strange fire before the LORD, which he commanded them not."* They are just out there because they are not a part of any local church. They are collections of people for many different places with many different spirits on them. Members do not have to have any commitment at all. All they want you to do is show up for rehearsal and sing with them. You can't sing with them without hooking up with them and you can't hook up with them without opening your womb. And it is really not a marriage if you do not receive some seed from them. In other words, there will be words from them going into your womb and then you get their spirit on you but you also have the spirit of your father. If you join that you collect all of that in your open womb. Now you wonder what is happening to you. You need to make sure that you function in some level of loyalty to your father and stay away from people who do not complement what my father is saying.

Declaration

Now you have to make a declaration of who you are with. Yon cannot be a part of something that you will not declare that you are connected to. Declaration is the next thing that you must do. You cannot be afraid to say who you are connected to.

Let us go to another scripture to see a different outlook that is positive and negative. *"And I, brethren, could not speak unto you as unto spiritual, but as unto carnal, even as unto babes in Christ. 2 I have fed you with milk, and not with meat: for hitherto ye were not able to bear it, neither yet now are ye able. 3 For ye are yet carnal: for whereas there is among you envying, and strife, and divisions, are ye not carnal, and walk as men? 4 For while one saith, I am of Paul; and another, I am of Apollos; are ye not carnal? 5 Who then is Paul, and who is Apollos, but ministers by whom ye believed, even as the Lord gave to every man?" (1 Cor 3:1-5)* There was nothing wrong with them connecting with Paul or Apollos, but they got their identity because of who Paul and Apollos were connected to. They got their identity because of God. But we know whose sprit is on you because of who you are connected to. You are not of your spiritual father, you are of God but we know whose spirit is on you.

Manifestation
And finally the manifestation comes. Something so strong came on them that would not cease because they become God breathed. You need to manifest what those who *prophesied, and did not cease* in Numbers 11 manifested. God took of Moses' spirit and breathed it on them. Who better to breathe Moses' spirit on them but the God who put it on Moses? Moses said that they could handle this and Moses and God knew that they could handle it even if those selected did not believe. Moses knew that they could

handle it and therefore, they needed to come into the reality of what Moses and God believed.

After my connection I need to make sure that I am declaring something for manifestation. I need something manifested in my life. What am I going to manifest, it is going to be what is on my father as long as I keep the connection pure. One of the problems that many of us have is that we do not really know what is on our father. We need to guard what is on our lives and not be so careless about our spiritual growth. When we have reached the manifestation of our father we start to teach like him, preach like him or whatever is on him comes on you. If you are my son you get to the place where you will not quit. You stop doing some things that used to be common in your life and you never realize that you have changed.

REPRODUCTION

Reproduction is the process of the father reproducing himself in the son through acts (The father has to be able to cut/circumcise the son) of:

* *Teaching*
* *Suffering*
* *Demonstration*
* *Lessons Learned*
* *Communications*
* *Reproving*
* *Mentoring*
* *Failures*
* *Discipline*
* *Rebuking*
* *Being*

Your spiritual father (pastor, leader, God's man, God's woman) has to serve his/her purpose in your life. *Spiritual Fathering is an apostolic function rendered to those in whom the Apostle/Prophet (set-gift) desires to reproduce himself.* If God has already done what He needs to do in me, it is my job to reproduce myself in those that He has put under my charge. While reproducing myself in you, I have to be sensitive to your purpose. God needs to see someone hand print on you. He needs to see that you are weaved from someone else's fabric. This process involves pouring the very life and nature of my own being into someone else in order for reproduction in the earth realm to take place. I need to put me in you. You should not have to go through what I went through. As a spiritual father, I went through everything that I have gone through so that I can hand it over to you on a silver platter. Everything that I have been through has already been processed and now the only thing that I need to do is to blow that in you. However, you must be receptive. It is my job to reproduce myself in you, but it is your job to receive that.

Let's see how God actually did this. We find that in Gen 2:7: *"And the LORD God formed man of the dust of the ground, and breathed into his nostrils the breath of life; and man became a living soul."* We see here that God formed man and breathed into him. The word breath is ruwach (roo'-akh) it means to breath into. So everything that God is was in man when He formed him. God put man together and saw man as what He wanted, but man had no life in him at this point. Remember that God said that He would make man according to Gen 1:26: *"And God said, Let us make man in our image, after our likeness:"* His image and after His likeness. In order to do this, God has to form (the word formed is an interesting word, it means put together) man. God looked at man and saw that this is what He wanted and breathed life into man because man needs to bear the image of God. Now after God has worked with the man and made him what He wanted him to be, man needs to make someone else like him. The person needs to be in his image and after his likeness. You need to be like somebody and not mind. Who are you like? Who can we say that we can liken you to?

Remember Jesus often said, I liken it to this or that. We can see one example of that in Mark 4:30: *"And he said, Where unto shall we liken the kingdom of God? or with what comparison shall we compare it?"* Who are you like? I watch people and I found that one of the ways that women come up with how they want their hair done is by looking in a book and finding something that they like. Then they take the book to their hairdresser and say, "Can you do this?" If you cannot do this, then I don't need you because you cannot do what I want. Remember that they get it out of a book and say I like that and I want my hair to look like that. Who are you like? You became who you are based on the people that influenced you to be like them. You picked up slang because you heard someone say it; you called someone "dog" because you heard someone say that. You came up with all of that because you like what you saw in someone. Now we know who you are like.

God breathed in them the "breath of like" so that they would be like Him. Who are you breathing on that is trying to be like you? Whether you are breathing something good or bad who are you breathing on? Most of our children are breathed on by us and they are trying to be like us because we breathed on them.

These are things to be learned not just victories, that what we aim for but your children don't just learn from your victories they learn from the stupid failures that we have had. We have to be man or woman enough to say I failed now you learn from that. Now our sons won't learn from it if we can't even acknowledge it. Some of the older generation use to say, "I am not always right but I am never wrong." This is not creating a model for anyone because now I don't know when you are wrong or when you are right. If I don't know when you are right I don't know what is right. We have to become a model for people to follow; this is the reason that I am so strong on order because it creates a model to follow. Without order people are confused about what is really right. Anybody that has children knows this. They will try to break your order, in other words they will pitch the mother against the father and the father against the mother. When one of them shows that they are the weaker link they will always go to the weaker link because they want to overthrow the order. So we as parents are not good models when we do that. Both parents need to display strong leadership in order to be a good model for the children.

REPLICATION

Replication is the process by which the son recognizes his own since of maturity and the degree of impartation that he has obtained. The son recognizes impartation when leadership is strong and has created the correct model. I was watching a television program where a counselor was helping a married couple. She asked them for one positive thing that they had learned from their parents and the husband said, "That is a tough one." That is very sad because you have lived with your parents all this time and you do not have one positive thing that you saw in your parents that you can use as a model. He could not think of one thing, not one. I wonder how many of us have a positive model of relationship. What are you going to replicate based on what you saw modeled. The purpose of this overall process is so that we can be reproductive. We want to reproduce what we have become.

Who is watching you and is now trying to model after you because you have such influence over their life. What are they going to model based on them watching you? What are they going to become? They are going to become whatever they see in you. This goes a lot further than just your children. There are people that see you every single day. They see you on the job, in the neighborhood, walking by the way and they are now going to be influenced to become what you are. Based on what you look like, what are they going to become? Jesus wanted to know, "Who do men say that I am and who do you say that I am?" Answering these questions is now going to give Jesus the answer as to what these disciples that have been with him all this time actually saw; how they interpreted what they saw on Him. In other words, am I being a wonderful role model to you and now you can model your life after me.

What are the people that you have influence over going to become? Are they going to become people who give up on life? Are they going to become people with a homosexual or lesbian spirit? Are they going to become doubters, liars, cheaters etc? What are they going to become based on what you show them? You have to understand replication and reproduction because people are going to model what they see in you. As an individual, you have influence over people's lives. You will be surprised who is watching you. You will be surprised who you have influence over. Why would people come to you if you do not have influence over them? Why do they keep showing up on your doorstep? It is because you have influence over them.

RELEASING

Releasing – the processing by which the son releases the anointing he has received through acts of engagement in ministry. The son stands to operate as the father did or does. The son experiences movement from the lesser to greater. The fact that you are in the presence of your father means you have an opportunity to receive the same anointing. The pastor or the set gift is not the only one with oil. When oil is poured on the head, it runs down; so the same oil that is on me is on my sons and I say to them, "Will you please get up and use that anointing." The reason they do not use it is because they believe that we have to determine if the oil is going to work. Let's see if we can make that make sense. Peter heals the sick, cast out devils, and was part of the process of raising the dead and different things like that. When Jesus got ready to be taken, we find that Peter still had murder in his heart, but God used him. If God can use a murderer, I think that you and I have a real good chance. We are giving more credit to who we are than we give to the anointing. Now, that is not a license to sin, it is not a license to do wrong, nor is it a license to be in error.

REIGNING

Reigning is the process of becoming a father to others - Operating in manifested sonship and pouring into others. Understand this, you have to become a type of father to someone, a type of model and become a father to sons. Every son grows up and becomes a father whether we like him or her or not. Can we be honest, we as parents do not always like who our children marry because the choice of a spouse is based on the intelligence of the chooser. Their choice is going to reflect their intelligence. We have to make sure that we are pouring into others. We have been poured into and now who are we pouring into? If you do not get to the point where you are pouring into someone you are going to die like a cockroach: he takes things in but has no way to get anything out. He does not leave dropping he just consumes until he dies. So you have to pour into someone and they are going to become like you. Some people have received all that they are going to receive. They are filled to capacity and now they have to find someone to pour into. Who is becoming better because you are pouring into them?

I want to reproduce myself into my sons. I am willing to do that based on what I have gone through, based on what I have accomplish and based on where I am right now. I am willing to reproduce that in my sons. They did not go through everything that I have been through, but I am willing to reproduce the results of the experiences I have received in them. But whether they are received or rejected, it is on them. I desire to reproduce myself in them, but I cannot make them receive. Receiving is on them. If they are not receiving, they have to change their minds. I cannot do that for them. They have to do that for themselves.

This process involves pouring the very life and nature of their own being into someone else in order for reproduction in the earth realm to take place. I have to pour everything that I am into my sons. That is one of the reasons I labor with them, I overlook stuff, I pray for them and I fast for them. It is expected that my sons will do the same for someone else. That is what Jesus said. When it comes down to our being an example, I need to become a portrait of what Jesus did for my sons and I need them to become a portrait of what they see in me. Fathers and sons have to love each other. As a spiritual father, I need to love my sons enough to correct them or encourage them. I understand one very important thing and that is if my father does not correct me he does not love me. I should be corrected when I am wrong. The only way I can avoid correction is to not be wrong in anything or to be perfect. If you really love someone you will correct them.

Your spiritual father has your words from God in his mouth. He is God's voice in the earth for you. And you are like Jesus' disciples when He asked them if they were leaving after the seventy left Him. Peter said to Jesus where shall we go in *John 6:66-69 From that time many of his disciples went back, and walked no more with him. 67 Then said Jesus unto the twelve, Will ye also go away? 68 Then Simon Peter answered him, Lord, to whom shall we go? thou hast the words of eternal life. 69 And we believe and are sure that thou art that Christ, the Son of the living God.* Even babies have to be cut from the umbilical cord when it is time to come to his/her mother and father. They have to separate from the afterbirth to get to their mother and father. They are connected to the new feeding place before they leave the former place. This was their place of feeding until it is time for them to born. After they are born, they have a new feeding place with their parents.

When it comes to leaving my spiritual father I don't even think about leaving him. I don't do that even in my thought life. You need to be receptive to what your father feeds you. Understand that everybody cannot feed you. You have to really get hooked up with your father spiritually. If you don't do that you just might get hooked up religiously. You may have a religious spirit on you, which mean you just need to say that you went to church. When you grow to a certain level of leadership it is not good enough. You are not satisfied with just saying that you went to church, your spirit man needs to know that you went to church. My spirit needs to know that I was there. Some of Jesus' disciples had a session with Jesus and they said this is good for us to be here. We see that in Mark 9:5: ***"And Peter answered and said to Jesus, Master, it is good for us to be here: ..."*** And another time that they said did not our hearts burn when He talked with us in Luke 24:32: ***"And they said one to another, Did not our heart burn within us, while he talked with us by the way, and while he opened to us the scriptures?"*** In other words, their spirit was refreshed. Sometimes we go from place to place to feed and our hearts does not burn at all, but we are too religious to realize that our heart did not burn. You must realize that you cannot get hooked up just anywhere. You cannot feed just anywhere; you must eat where God told you to feed.

Let's take a look at this in 2 *Kings 2:1-6*

"And it came to pass, when the LORD would take up Elijah into heaven by a whirlwind, that Elijah went with Elisha from Gilgal. 2 And Elijah said unto Elisha, Tarry here, I pray thee; for the LORD hath sent me to Bethel. And Elisha said unto him, As the LORD liveth, and as thy soul liveth, I will not leave thee. So they went down to Bethel. 3 And the sons of the prophets that were at Bethel came forth to Elisha, and said unto him, Knowest thou that the LORD will take away thy master from thy head to day? And he said, Yea, I know it; hold ye your peace. 4 And Elijah said unto him, Elisha, tarry here, I pray thee; for the LORD hath sent me to Jericho. And he said, As the LORD liveth, and as thy soul liveth, I will not leave thee. So they came to Jericho. 5 And the sons of the prophets that were at Jericho came to Elisha, and said unto him, Knowest thou that the LORD will take away thy master from thy head to day? And he answered, Yea, I know it; hold ye your peace. 6 And Elijah said unto him, Tarry, I pray thee, here; for the LORD hath sent me to Jordan. And he said, As the LORD liveth, and as thy soul liveth, I will not leave thee. And they two went on." 2 Kings 2:1-6

We see from this passage that they went from Gilgal, Bethel, Jericho and Jordan. Every one of these places actually means something. Let's go to Gilgal first, Gilgal comes from a Hebrew word Gllgal which means rolling away. This leaves us with the understanding of circumcision.

Elisha's objective was to follow Elijah to Gilgal and remain there until all of the unneeded parts of his life were taken away. His spiritual father's purpose at that particular point was to make sure that he cut off of him the unneeded parts. Think about that a minute, what is it that we need cut from our lives that would make us better? The next thing that we need to ask ourselves is how well do we receive correction? Can your leader really correct you and you embrace the correction? You have to understand that this is a part of the overall process of growth. We have to be corrected if we are going to grow. Therefore, if we are going to grow we have to have a Gilgal experience in our overall spiritual process of growth. What part of your life that you say that you need to cut off right now so that you can grow to the next place? If you have something that needs to be cut off, have you positioned yourself so that it can happen? Have you identified the things that are attached to you that you know you need to get rid of because they hinder you from growing to this next place?

What is the purpose of being circumcised? It makes sure that you are going to have a good opportunity for reproduction. There are things that we allow to stay attached to us that cut off our ability to produce. Given the fact that we have these things that keep us from being productive, are we willing to cut them off so that we can be productive? Or do we love these things so much that we are willing to sacrifice our level of production just to hold onto that?

The next place that they went to was Bethel which is the place of God's presence. The only way that we can come into the full presence of God is to go through this place of being circumcised. We cannot avoid being circumcised if we want the presence of God.

In that process you will find that there are things and also people that you have to cut off because the presence of God means more to you and I than people. Are there people that you are holding onto so tight that it is cutting off the life source of the presence of God? Let's think about manners and customs of this particular time period when Elijah and Elisha were in operation. Where did they come from? Why was he there (at that particular place) in 1 Kings 19:14: *"And he said, I have been very jealous for the LORD God of hosts: because the children of Israel have forsaken thy covenant, thrown down thine altars, and slain thy prophets with the sword; and I, even I only, am left; and they seek my life, to take it away."* One of the things that he was confronted with is Jezebel. This is letting us in on some particular things that were very prevalent in that time period: Prophets were being killed, they were covenant breakers, prophets were asked to cut down the groves (this was a heavy level of perversion in that day just like it is in our day) prophets had to deal with things like this and that is why they were killing them. They were engaged in different levels of perversion. They had to deal with homosexuality and things like that. This is not something new this was happening back then. Things like that cause the hand of God to move against people.

If the prophets were going to move from Gilgal to Bethel it meant that they were going to have to cut down some of this stuff in order to get through. The prophet was getting a sense of what was in the heart of God in terms of the jealousy and dealing with the perverted ways of the people of God. God would send the prophet in there and say tear it all down. Remember this, one of the things that will cause the hand of God to begin to move against the people that He so desires to bless is the spirit of perversion.

Sin is one thing but when we operate on a perverted level that is an abomination against God, in other words it moves against the original order of God. Now when we justify our perverse ways then the hand of God has to move against that. God says regardless of anything I have to come after that person, I have to come after that generation or I have to come after that nation because they are voluntarily on purpose becoming perverse (operating outside of God's original order). Elisha had not been hanging around prophets up to this point and some of this stuff Elisha must be cleansed from Elisha in order for him to take on the next assignment which is the place of God's presence (Bethel). He now goes from the place of God's presence to determine if he received the first level of the stuff that was designed to come on him. The first level of the stuff that was to come on him was going to be proven once he gets to the place called Jericho.

Jericho is a place of conquest. That is the reasons that you do not walk through Jericho unless you have had the unneeded parts stripped off of you and you now have God's presence on you. Remember the man going to Jericho in Luke 10:30: *"And Jesus answering said, A certain man went down from Jerusalem to Jericho, and fell among thieves, which stripped him of his raiment, and wounded him, and departed, leaving him half dead."* Jericho was a rough place; it was not the place that you wanted to be caught without the presence of God on you. Now the Good Samaritan was on the same road: *"But a certain Samaritan, as he journeyed, came where he was: and when he saw him, he had compassion on him,"* (Luke 10:33) So what was the difference? The Good Samaritan had the presence of God on him but the man traveling did not. One had the defenses of God with him and the other did not, so the one that fell prey to this had to lean on the grace of the Good Samaritan. Now we go from Gilgal, to

Bethel, to Jericho to the ultimate testing place to see if you have the spirit of your father on you which is the Jordan. Another observation is that as he goes to each place there were voices that he was hearing. There were voices in speaking to Elisha everywhere he went during this process saying *"Knowest thou that the LORD will take away thy master from thy head to day" (2 Kings 2:3) "And the sons of the prophets that were at Bethel came forth to Elisha, and said unto him, Knowest thou that the LORD will take away thy master from thy head today? And he said, Yea, I know it; hold ye your peace." (2 Kings 2:5) "And the sons of the prophets that were at Jericho came to Elisha, and said unto him, Knowest thou that the LORD will take away thy master from thy head today? And he answered, Yea, I know it; hold ye your peace."* Elisha said *"Yea, I know it; hold ye your peace."* In other words don't keep telling me that I already know that. Now understand this all of the companies were not going to follow Elijah because they knew that he was going to be taken away from them so they did not want to get too close to him. In other words, let's not get too close to people because this one too may be taken away. Isn't that a trap? Elisha says I know that he is going to be taken away, I am sensitive to that but we are only in the season that is going to happen we are not in the time that's designed to happen.

"Let's take a look at what happens next. And fifty men of the sons of the prophets went, and stood to view afar off: and they two stood by Jordan. 8 And Elijah took his mantle, and wrapped it together, and smote the waters, and they were divided hither and thither, so that they two went over on dry ground. 9 And it came to pass, when they were gone over, that Elijah said unto Elisha, Ask what I shall do for thee, before I be taken away from thee. And Elisha said, I pray thee, let a double portion of thy spirit be upon me. 10 And he said, Thou hast asked a hard thing: nevertheless, if thou see me when I am taken

from thee, it shall be so unto thee; but if not, it shall not be so. 11 And it came to pass, as they still went on, and talked, that, behold, there appeared a chariot of fire, and horses of fire, and parted them both asunder; and Elijah went up by a whirlwind into heaven."
2 Kings 2:7-11.

You have to understand the longevity that Elisha had. God looks for people who have staying power so that he can put the fullness of what He has on them. God has no problem doing that as long as we have staying power. God does not want to take the spirit that was on Moses and put it on people that didn't have staying power. So God says to Moses, "I need you to look among the people who you know, not just people who you think have a call on their lives." God asked Moses to choose people that he knew to be elders that were also elders in deed. *"And the LORD said unto Moses, Gather unto me seventy men of the elders of Israel, whom thou knowest to be the elders of the people, and officers over them; and bring them unto the tabernacle of the congregation, that they may stand there with thee."* (Num 11:16) God told Moses to bring them and He was going to put the spirit that was on him on them. *"And I will come down and talk with thee there: and I will take of the spirit which is upon thee, and will put it upon them; and they shall bear the burden of the people with thee, that thou bear it not thyself alone."* (Num 11:17) What God was telling Moses is that He was duplicating him in order to expand his reach. Do you have saying power that will enable you to produce whatever your leader produces? Do you have to bring people to your leader in order to get them set free? You should be able to do that yourself. The same anointing that is on your leader is on you, but you have to embrace that. That is one of the reasons Jesus asked His disciples, "Who do men say that I am and also who do you say that I am?" *"And it came to pass, as he was alone praying, his disciples were with him: and he asked them, saying, Whom say the people that I am? 20 He said unto them, But whom say ye that I am? Peter answering said, The Christ of God." (Luke 9:18, 20)* Because I need to determine if God has already put my spirit on you, Jesus is saying that we need to see eye to eye, because if we are not seeing eye to eye then we do not have the same spirit. Now because we are in the arena of the same spirit and anointing that means that we have the same ability. Are you walking under the same cloud that God has place over your house of God?

Are we agreeing because agreement takes place on purpose? I purposely agree with the word, but there is something on the inside of me at various times that wants to disagree with the word. The reason is because my flesh would like to have its way sometimes. How about yours? Does your flesh ever want to have its way? Think about your flesh, does anybody ever get on your nerves so that you want to have a real good argument that day? Have you reached a level where you are not even tempted to argue? Your flesh wants to disagree that this is the way of God, but now can't fool you enough to do it. So you on purpose agree God this is your word this is what I agree with! Regardless of how we feel the Bible says husbands ought to honor their wives as the weaker vessel. *"Likewise, ye husbands, dwell with them according to knowledge, giving honor unto the wife, as unto the weaker vessel, and as being heirs together of the grace of life; that your prayers be not hindered." (1 Peter 3:7)* If you are a husband, is there ever a time where you get angry and do not want to agree with her and honor her? But guess what?

That is what the Bible says. That is what the word of God says, so husbands are to handle them with care and honor them as the weaker vessel. Not that she is a weak vessel, the word says as a weaker vessel. This does not mean that they are weak, they are just weaker or at least they are supposed to be if the relationship is properly aligned. The word assumes that the husband is stronger than the wife that he marries. I know that is not always the case. Regardless of what you think, if you are a husband you are to honor her as the weaker vessel.

Now Elijah and Elisha go across the Jordan then Elijah spins around and says to Elisha, "Ask what I shall do for you before I am taken away?" *"And it came to pass, when they were gone over, that Elijah said unto Elisha, Ask what I shall do for thee, before I be taken away from thee. And Elisha said, I pray thee, let a double portion of thy spirit be upon me."* *(2 Kings 2:9)* Elijah is now having him to engage, having him to look at him eye to eye. Elijah is saying Elisha I need you to look at me eye to eye because you have always related to me as master. Elisha had always related to Elijah as master and there is a rule that if the person is your master you do not look at them eye to eye. But if the person is your father there is no problem looking them eye to eye and that is what he meant when he said if you see me when I am taken away from you, you have it. *"And he said, ... if thou see me when I am taken from thee, it shall be so unto thee; but if not, it shall not be so."(2 Kings 2:10)* So when he was taken up Elisha did not say "master, master", he said, "my father, my father" which was an indication that I have seen you, I looked into your eyes, now watch this because this is the thing that we are going to have to understand. The word says that the light of the body is the eye. *"The light of the body is the eye: if therefore thine eye be single, thy whole body shall be full of light." (Matt 6:22)* Then the light that is in Elijah came into Elisha.

What is it that caused Elisha to get to that place because everybody does not get to that place? You have to earn the right to look eye to eye. In other words, you have to go to Gilgal and accept the correction in Gilgal and then go into the presence of God, Bethel. Afterword, go on to the place of testing, Jericho and then go on to the Jordan. Please understand once you get on the other side of the Jordan you have to have caught what you saw your father do because now you have to do it.

Do you see this process? Remember that it is a process of *Recognition, Reception, Reproduction, Replication, Releasing and Reigning.* You have to get to a point where you are reigning the same way that Elisha reigned. You ought to look like you are in charge. If you are heading anything you ought to look like you are in charge. People should not come and wonder who is in charge here? I talk with leaders and there are times when certain leaders have to leave where they are because people see them in the down line as if they are the pastor. That is because there is weak leadership leading in that particular group.

NOTE

The Prophet and Deliverance

Within the general makeup of the prophet is the gift of discernment. This is, or should be, a gift that flows out of the prophetic person. The gift of discerning spirits, along with the other eight gifts of the Spirit, should be manifested in the life of the prophet, the prophetic minister, and occasionally those who function in prophetic gifting. It is the gift of discerning of spirits that will enable the prophet to see supernaturally, the plans, purpose, and workings of the enemy and its force. Also, the gift of discerning of spirits, will give the prophet the ability to see in the realm of the spirit, in order to clearly understand the maneuvering, and the functioning of the spirit that is in operation, and that is giving physical manifestation at that time.

We need to look beyond what we see, in order to recognize the plan, purpose and workings of the enemy. We do this with the gift of discerning of spirits. The enemy has a plan to talk you out of obeying God and to start doubting God. The enemy wants to stop the flow of what God is doing. The gift of discerning of spirits is not discerning what people are doing, but discerning the operation of spirits. God will reveal particular spirits, and not just tell people's business. Sometimes people are afraid to come into the presence of a prophet; because they have the misunderstanding that God is going to tell the prophet all of their business and he or she is going to tell everybody. This is especially true if they know that they have some things in their lives that they need to change. God is not a gossip, and what He reveals He intends to heal. Prophets and some prophetic people are able to discern particular spirits, seeing into the realm of the spirit, and be able to know the plan, purpose and workings of the enemy. And they can attack these plans, purposes and workings of the enemy and not people.

"To another the working of miracles; to another prophecy, to another discerning of spirits, to another divers kinds of tongues and to another the interpretation of tongues."
I Corinthians 12:10

In Mark 9: 4-29 there is an account of a physical manifestation of a deaf and dumb spirit that had possessed the young boy who was brought to the Lord Jesus by his father for deliverance. Let us take a look at some possible manifestations of a deaf and dumb spirit, and how it would manifest itself at particular levels of oppression and possession. This example in Mark 9 is possession. But this spirit may not always be in the form of possession. It may come in the form of oppression. Possession is the total control by a demonic force, over an individual's soul (mind, will, emotion and intellect). Oppression is a force that would come against or attack the mind and/or the flesh. Oppression works from the outside. It is more emotional than spiritual.

It is the role and responsibility of the prophet, to recognize and/or identify the various levels of spiritual and demonic influence, within the congregation.

It is important not to call what may be a work of the flesh, demonic or what may be demonic, a work of the flesh. We must identify what the works of the flesh are and must not attempt to cast out what is not demonic.

The person operating in the works of the flesh (Galatians 5:17-21) is not necessarily demonic. The individual must take authority and control over their own flesh, bringing it into subjection to their recreated or born-again spirit. This begins the developing of babes in Christ, versus someone who continually walks in the flesh. The prophet would have to discern this area, because of his authority to correct and/ or chastise the body.

Those that are babes will find themselves wrestling with their flesh. Once again, this does not mean that it is a demonic influence.

Recognizing Demonic Influence

We must be able to recognize the various stages of demonic influence. There are six stages.

> 1. **Regression:** *Regression is to withdraw or to back away from.* We should be able to discern this stage within the midst of our congregation. People who begin to become isolated from the body are in the stage of regression.
>
> One of the ways to identify people who are headed to the back door of the church, is by their acts of regression toward the back of the church. This demonic activity causes them to be incapable of

communicating. You have to go after them. You will notice that they will begin to change their seat from wherever they normally sit, to a little farther back, each time they come to church. The next time they come, they stop talking to people, and will not say anything to anyone. They are literally backing their way out of the back door. This is the time when you go after them, because you recognize the signs and they are not able to communicate with you. These are the beginning stages of demonic influence of regression.

When is this regression and when is this prophetic preparation?

Regression does not allow you to interact with others. However, regressing prophetically will not prevent your interaction, but will cause conflict in forcing interaction, because of your season.

Regression also has a prophetic side. Regression is a prophetic act when you sense in your spirit that God is doing something with you prophetically, that you cannot have interference with. At this time you begin to regress, and you really need to do that. You need to get away from people who will interfere with your process of receiving from God at this time. This does not mean that you are angry with anyone; you can talk to people and communicate with people. There are no demonic forces involved, because you are not hindered from communicating; you are choosing to separate yourself, so that you can receive from God.

2. Suppression: *Suppression is manifested from lack of joy.* A person begins to hide his or her feelings and is unable to express joy.

To suppress is to keep from being revealed, or to inhibit the expression of something. The prophet must be mindful of what he talks about or confesses.

Men do this from time to time, especially married men. This is a dangerous thing to do, because this act of suppression, leads you to the next stage of depression. This demonic influence is leading you to a place of losing control and that is not what God wants to happen to us. Most healthy people just go off every time something happens; they do not suppress anything.

Prophetically we use suppression to control the flow of information. This is prophetic preparation.

Suppression is different. Suppression is denying what they feel.

3. Depression: *Depression is a broken spirit.* People are not able to overcome the things in their lives. God has been speaking to you through all of these previous stages. Now He is saying, "Come out of this." At this stage, you have started to follow the demon out of the presence of God, and God wants you to come out now, because this leads you to the next phase of oppression. You cannot carry some things, because you are not designed to do that. God wants to carry that care for you. The only thing that you are designed to carry is the word of God and the glory of God.

If not arrested, caught or put in check at this point, depression will lead to oppression, which opens the door to possession.

Depression is a period of drastic decline. There is that time when the prophet goes into a desert place, but never a drastic decline.

4. Oppression: *Oppression describes one who is weighed down with the cares of this world.* Oppressed people lack victory. At this stage, people cannot remember any of their victories in their lives. This shuts down the voice of God.

Oppression is to keep down by unjust use of authority, or to weigh heavily on the mind or spirit (I Corinthians 7:37; 2 Corinthians 9:7 NIV or NASB).

The prophetic side of oppression is called discipline.

Your flesh is being oppressed. Discipline is training expected to produce a specific character or pattern. School is the place of discipline and challenge.

5. Obsession: *Obsession describes one who lacks reality.* Obsessed individuals become focused on one particular sin in their life. At this stage, they are not functioning the way that God created them.

Obsession is defined as a compulsive, often unreasonable idea or emotion, or an irresistible impulse to act on an unreasonable idea, problem or thing.

This quality should be on the prophet in a positive sense. It should happen in a time of preparation.

6. Possession: *A person experiencing possession is someone who comes under total control of a demonic force.*

In our prophetic preparatory period, we should come under the control of the Holy Spirit, which involves being totally submitted to Him (I Corinthians 16:14-16).

They have addicted themselves to the ministry of the saints.

The Spirit of Perversion

Homosexuals are bound with the spirit of perversion. The word perversion means to deviate from the original form. There are men who are bound by that spirit having never entered into a homosexual relationship. Likewise, people who are bound with that spirit, make a choice to leave their natural use.

The first five of these stages are mental and emotional harassment by the enemy. The sixth is spiritual, ***a total*** *yielding* of the person's soul to a demonic force. All of these stages, through the gift of discerning of spirits, can be discerned, and the person can be delivered.

The Prophet's Role in Discernment

Through the prophet's spiritual insight, his or her ability to discern spiritual influence is great. Within the prophet's role and responsibilities in ministry, there will be times during impartation, that it is necessary for him to be cognizant of various levels of demonic influence, oppression and/or possession. The prophet may, from time to time, discern, cast out and/or deliver an individual from whatever level of demonic influence present.

Particular Spirits and How They Manifest

Mark 1:21-28 A Religious Spirit: The manifestation of this unclean spirit seemed to have a revelation of who Jesus was and a religious knowledge that would allow him to fit in with most religious people.

The remedy: Jesus prophetically discerned the spirit and its function and commanded it to hold its peace and come out of the man.

Mark 5:1-19 A Spirit of Insanity: The manifestation of this unclean spirit was able to tap into a portion of this man's mind, and cause him to have incredible strength. This is a man who manifested multiple personalities, through the influence of a demonic spirit, that brought much damage to his body. But, at a spare break from demonic activity, he in the presence of Jesus, fell down and worshipped Him. This was a clear indication that showed an act on the man's part that he wanted to be delivered.

The scriptures can help us identify the difference between a demonic spirit and a sickness. When Jesus was in the presence of sickness, there was not a spiritual or physical reaction. But when He was in the presence of demonic influence, there was a manifestation or a reaction within the person. Both physical and spiritual are present. The demonic spirit responds with a physical manifestation.

The gift of discerning of spirits is one of the many gifts within the body of Christ. *"Now ye are the body of Christ and members in particular." (1 Cor 12:27* Are you sure that you can recognize "the realms of prophecy?"

Order Form

Another Touch of Glory Ministries/Press

2760 Crain Highway
Waldorf, MD 20601
301- 843-9267 • Fax 240- 585-7093
www.bishoprswalkerproducts.com
email: admin@bishoprswalker.com

Items Ordered:
Name

Title   Date

Church/Ministry

Address

City   State   Zip

Daytime Phone   Email

Items Ordered:

Description	CD	DVD	Qty
Total			
Raising Prophets of Character Book $14.95			
School of the Prophets 21-week Course			
Volume 1-3	$30	$60	
Volume 4	$20	$40	
Extended Favor of God (6-CDs)		$30	$60
The Power of First Fruit Offering (6-CDs)	$30		$60
The Art of Tongues Book $ 9.99			
Raising Prophets Prayer Devotional $14.99			

Creating Habits for a Functional Life		$14.99
The Father Son Encounter		$14.95
The Fundamentals of Faith (6-CDs)	$50	
The Power of First Fruit Offering (6-CDs)	$30	$60

Shipping Information:
Add $4 for Priority Mail first item
$1 per additional item
MD add 5% sales tax

Method of Payment:

Please charge my:

VISA □ AMEX
Card Number:

Total price of items
Add shipping charge
Tax (if applicable)
Total Amount Enclosed

□ Discover □ MasterCard □

Exp Date: MM/YY □□ □□

Signature (as shown on credit card):

□   Check or Money Order

For Speaking Engagements contact:
Office of Bishop Administrative Staff
301-843-9267

www.ingramcontent.com/pod-product-compliance
Lightning Source LLC
LaVergne TN
LVHW051517080426
835509LV00017B/2087